# Catch Me
# a Catch

# Catch Me a Catch

### Chronicles of a
### Modern-Day Matchmaker

**Leora Hoffman**

BookBound Media, LLC

ISBN-13: 978-0-9989652-2-2 (trade paper)
ISBN-10: 0-9989652-2-7 (trade paper)
ISBN-13: 978-0-9989652-3-9 (e-Pub)
ISBN-10: 0-9989652-3-5 (e-Pub)

Publisher: BookBound Media, LLC
         www.bookboundmedia.com

Cover design by Miladinka Milic
Author photo by Hilary Schwab
Interior design and formatting by Tonya Woodworth

For Stuart: Rest in peace.

# CONTENTS

# FOREWORD

*W*e've all known the pleasure of watching someone who has special skills do that thing they do. For eight years, I've had the privilege to watch Leora work her magic up close and personal: To see couples brought together by an intuition that, to the untrained eye, can seem counter-intuitive. To see a comprehensive, personal approach to matchmaking that is as much or more about consultation than it is finding a date for a client. To hear the wisdom of counseling patience and of giving the other person a chance, and to thereby give yourself another chance.

We live in a time in which we have seemingly unlimited choices but, paradoxically, the cultural gravity seems to pull us toward greater isolation. Technology has created as many problems as it has solved. By employing a time-honored tradition, matchmaking, in a modern way, Leora exerts her own gravity and brings people together. It's a gift, and we're fortunate to have her share it with us.

In this book, Leora lays out the joys, sorrows, and pitfalls of twenty-first-century dating, especially for those in their fifties, sixties, and seventies, and she gives wise advice about how to manage those dynamics. As you'll see, she gets it! I believe her ability to consult with and advise clients who confide in her regarding these issues as their relationships begin and evolve is her greatest strength. She has an innate understanding of social dynamics and thirty years of matchmaking experience to inform her suggestions. And she knows when to be gentle and when to push. Those who work with her quickly find that they're in capable and trusted hands.

I'm a psychologist, so I've seen a lot of the issues Leora lays out here and how they play out for better or for worse. I want to underscore some of her themes that I believe are most relevant to finding and nurturing a sustaining relationship.

Anyone who's in a good relationship will tell you that they require work. They aren't born fully formed, like Athena from the head of Zeus. Each of us is growing and changing, month by month, year by year, even when we're no longer kids. And each of us brings two contradictory states to a new relationship: an adolescent's dream of perfection and an adult's personal history and preferences, or what some like to call "baggage." Reconciling these dreams and differences with one's partner, with respect and kindness, is an ongoing task. But by doing so, a couple achieves something greater than infatuation: comfort and joy, a feeling that each is enriched by the other.

I see people fall into three traps when they pursue or consider pursuing a relationship: being too quick to dismiss a potential partner, holding the partner to impossible standards, or deciding not to try at all. Though seemingly disparate, the three approaches have a common underpinning: the fear of taking a risk and the corresponding inability to open oneself to new possibilities. The fear is natural, but it must be overcome. This is where a strong support system—friends, family and Leora—comes in, people who will support and encourage you moving forward. And if necessary, counseling with an experienced therapist can help.

When a person is ready to take the risk, the cultivation of two traits—patience and being willing and able to compromise—goes a long way in bringing a relationship to fruition. Our ever-faster world, driven by continuous technological development, erodes patience; it's a dilemma that pervades our lives. But if you're going to focus your increasingly limited patience on one thing, let it be the patience to allow your interaction with a potential partner to unfold. Don't preempt; see where it goes. And the path requires compromise, to be able to determine the difference between what's really important for you and what may be a tired habit, to see what it would be like to do things differently, to meet in the middle. But if, after being given your patience, your potential partner can't compromise, head elsewhere.

To achieve your goals, you also need tools. Leora lays out plenty here. I'll emphasize three: communication, humor, and, if necessary, couples counseling. When in doubt, communicate! Don't assume, communicate! Yes, sometimes it can be difficult or awkward, but the goal is to truly know the other person. You can't know if you don't ask, and they can't know you if you don't tell. (The inverse of that proposition—don't ask, don't tell—should sound familiar to most of you. I always wanted to thank the Clinton administration for providing a motto for the dysfunctional family coat of arms.) And let me second one of Leora's pet peeves: for anything other than logistical purposes, *talk, don't text*. Text misunderstandings, which occur all the time, can be the death of a budding relationship. Humor, done with appropriate kindness and self-deprecation, lubricates communication and gracefully acknowledges that we're all flawed. Also, it's sexy. Yes, Leora is beautiful, accomplished, honorable, and kind, but I most love her sense of humor . . . and, even more, that she laughs at all my jokes. Lastly, when you and your partner seemingly hit a wall that communication and advice from friends and family can't surmount, see an experienced couples counselor. As Leora tells you in this book, we have done so, and we've benefitted greatly from it.

—Dr. Jim Fleming

# ACKNOWLEDGMENTS

$\mathcal{M}$y journey as a matchmaker has taken many twists and turns. Without the advice and support of so many people, I would have never begun a career as matchmaker, let alone written this book. Firstly, I am grateful to my sister, Dr. Evelyn Rappoport, for giving me the inspiration to start a matchmaking business in the DC area, as I struggled to figure out my next career move.

The idea to write this book came from Arnold Sanow, MBA, whom I consulted in 1989 for a business plan when I first explored the possibility of starting a matchmaking company. He advised me to write a book, which would support my efforts in marketing my services. At that time, I had no idea what to write, so this goal lay dormant for thirty years until I acquired enough material and experience to comfortably write about.

I am eternally grateful to my late friend Stuart Chang Berman, a talented author himself, criminologist, and gourmet chef, who encouraged me to write about the stories I would regale him with during our many hours spent together commiserating about being newly divorced and back in the singles' world. His untimely death gave me the impetus to organize my thoughts and write my stories as a tribute to his love and support.

Of course, none of this would have been possible without my clients who trusted me with their stories and invested in my services. I am especially grateful to my many friends who encouraged me to persevere during the many difficult periods I endured in my life and in my business development, namely Cathy and Steve Polin, Agnes Aranyi, Barbara Kaufman, Marty Blumsack, Victor Goodman, Jonathan Rose, Paulette Hurwitz, Marsha Stein, Emunah Herzog, Rabbi Tamara Miller, Malka Wasser, Irit Dagan, Cindy Blond, Rob Goldstein, Penny Kahn, Sandy Feldman, Betty Sinowitz, Judith Asner, Barbara Champaloux, Harriet Kerwin, and Jane Weissman.

Thank you to Sylvia Rosenwasser for your continued prayers on my behalf for the success of my business, as well as in my personal life, which have indeed been answered.

Thank you to my networkers Rhona Reiss, Judith Beltz, Alysa Dortort, Deborah Srabstein, Shari Solomon, Roya Vasseghi, and Gloria Goldman. Without you I could never have made as many matches as I have. Thank you also to my matchmaking affiliates Options, Sweet Beginnings, a Little Nudge, and DC Matchmaking for your collaboration and support.

I am grateful to the following professionals: Buck Downs for your masterful editing and encouragement during the writing of my first draft; Linda Schenk for your online marketing, website expertise, and support; Rabbi Bernice Weiss, a friend and accomplished author, who referred me to my current editor, Tonya Woodworth. Without each of your expertise and support, I could not have written this book.

Tonya, thank you for your initial positive take on my draft and for your devotion to this project, support, expertise, and encouragement for me to persevere in the face of my doubts, other responsibilities, and life challenges.

I am grateful to my family for their love and support through everything. My parents instilled a drive in me to accomplish everything I set out to do, and this book serves as a tribute to them as well. My children, Elana and Adam, have always given me a purpose even when I couldn't see one myself. Thank you Elana for your encouragement to tell my story and to speak my truth.

My own story is a testament to the benefit of having a matchmaker. I am forever grateful to Deborah and Spencer Ward for your wisdom, insight, and perseverance in matching me with Jim.

Finally, I am grateful to my husband, Jim, who has made this journey worthwhile. When we met, I had no idea what an impact you would have on my life, and how, through your love and devotion, I would finally experience a sense of security, inner peace, and happiness I never thought possible.

# INTRODUCTION

*R*elationships have always fascinated me. Since becoming a matchmaker over thirty years ago, my sole intention has been to help others find love, regardless of my personal circumstances. My own journey has been an intense, often turbulent, yet ultimately healing one that has weaved its way throughout my practice over the years.

Hollywood's depiction of instant chemistry, courtship, and deep, abiding love is a notion that pervades our culture. As a result, hopeless romantics fervently aspire to be swept away by love. But it doesn't always happen that way. If I have learned anything, it is that the magic of love can emerge in a myriad of ways. In fact, some of the best, most fulfilling relationships start out quite differently.

I have been very fortunate to make my living helping people find and maintain love. My former career as an attorney for over twenty years in several fields—including criminal defense, domestic violence, and child protection—provided me with a healthy balance as I juggled two professions. Both worlds have been invaluable in deepening my understanding of human needs and frailties. I have also become smarter and more empathetic in my work as a matchmaker, and I deeply value the trust each client has placed in me. Along with their commitment to the process, this trust has inspired me to dig even deeper within myself to find their perfect match.

From the time I became single four years into my matchmaking practice, I maintained a strict boundary between my business and personal life. I chose not to date anyone I worked with and not to work with anyone I had dated. This made it even harder for me to meet someone. I had no idea that this career path would work against me in my own dating life or that men might be put off by my profession.

Through the trials and triumphs depicted in this book, this is the story of the clients I have successfully matched, tried to match, coached, and sometimes disappointed. This is also a memoir of my own quest to find Mr. Right and how my business has both buoyed and burdened my search. In keeping with the coaching aspect of my practice, each story reflects the relationship advice I've tried to impart upon my clients along the way. Some were more receptive than others. While the anecdotes in this book are all based on actual events, in the interest of confidentiality, names and some basic facts have been changed. Each story's premise, however, has stayed the same.

## CHAPTER ONE

# My Last First Date

*N*oting the irony of the entryway, I walked through the revolving door to a popular neighborhood restaurant called Founding Farmers to meet Jim. The door seemed to be an apt symbol of my dating life, given that I had been on dozens of dates, mostly through online introductions, since my second divorce twelve years earlier. This one, however, was different.

Good friends introduced us, and they knew us both very well. The wife was my good friend and a couples therapist, so I trusted her judgment. The husband was Jim's old friend and work colleague who had seen Jim through the loss of his wife six years earlier. As such, he was heavily invested in helping Jim move on.

The couple told Jim that I was a lawyer working for the DC attorney general in the Child Protection Division. They told me that Jim was chief psychologist in a treatment-based correctional facility in Maryland, so we were well matched professionally, which was a good start. They had worked incessantly for two years to get us together. Finally, we agreed. The time had come.

I saw Jim wave to me as I approached the bar and immediately felt a mixture of nervousness and resignation. We had exchanged photos, so I knew who to look for. Unfortunately, this made things a bit more awkward for me initially because I didn't feel that he was my type. It was a visceral response on my part that I tried to put aside in the interest of keeping an open mind. While I wanted to like him, I had my doubts, especially after our initial phone call, which had not gone all that well. On top of that, he had described himself through several e-mails in terms that I didn't find all that appealing.

So here we were, Jim having obliged his friend to meet me and me feeling so tired of dating that I had almost resigned myself to accepting my fate of remaining single. After all, I was blessed in so many other ways. I had two children who were my pride and joy, despite having raised them under highly stressful conditions. I had pulled myself together after two divorces, built an interesting career, had a loving circle of family and friends, managed to travel often, and generally had a happy life. I finally concluded that I would be okay without a man, but in my heart of hearts, I longed for the love that was missing from my life.

To my surprise, I found Jim charming, wickedly funny, and incredibly sharp. About halfway into my first glass of wine, I became increasingly engaged in the conversation and intrigued by this man. His journey had been a heart-wrenching one, and he openly shared his experience with complete honesty, without becoming melodramatic or overemotional. I admired his devotion to his late wife, whose illness had dragged on for many years. Since then, Jim had tried online dating, and we exchanged anecdotes about some of those experiences, laughing at the various characters we'd encountered and at ourselves for handling some of the those situations so pathetically.

Once I gathered up the courage, I told him that I was a professional matchmaker. Jim paused and asked, "Well, what the hell are you doing here?" I couldn't blame him for asking. He must have thought that I'd have the "pick of the litter" from my population of single male clients and didn't need to be on a blind date. My cheeks burned as I explained to him how my professional ethics prevented me from dating my own clients; therefore, it had been even harder for me to meet a quality man. Jim understood right away and tried to make me feel better by reassuring me that he felt awkward about dating, too, and wished there were an easier way for him as well.

The evening sped by as fast as the wine flowed, and we lingered over our salads for hours. I found myself confiding in this man for some unknown reason, sharing things about my life I would have never disclosed on a first date. He responded to the trust that I had placed in him and reciprocated. It was touching. We also laughed often and easily together and discovered that we shared a similar sense of humor and skeptical outlook on life. Before we knew it, it was 11:00 p.m. on a "school night," so Jim asked for the check, which I was pleased about, and we called it a night.

As we exited the restaurant into the cold March night, I realized just how much fun I'd had, absent any flirtation on either of our parts, unlike so many dates I'd experienced in the past. Standing outside awkwardly and trembling in the bitter-cold wind, neither of us knew exactly how to end the evening. I wasn't sure what I really wanted but thanked him politely and said that it was nice to have finally met him. He made no move to give me a goodbye hug or kiss. Instead, he said the same, and we parted ways. During my drive home, I played the evening over again in my head. "That was by far the most interesting and substantive conversation I've ever had on a first date," I thought, "But who knows whether I'll ever see him again."

I resumed the frenetic activity of my life, and after five days, I had not heard from Jim. "Well, that was that," I thought. By the end of the week, however, I was surprised to get an e-mail from him. He wrote that while he had enjoyed our conversation very much and "could see how we could build on that," he was "unsure about the chemistry between us." My ego was somewhat stung by his lack of passion toward me. I didn't know how to respond. Part of me thought, "You're the guy. Why are you putting this on me? If you like me, then just ask me out again!" On the other hand, I found myself happy to hear from him again and respected his honesty.

> **I had witnessed many couples work out after an initial period of uncertainty.**

Was I interested in seeing him again? The question brought to bear years of experience coaching clients in my matchmaking practice. I had witnessed many couples work out after an initial period of uncertainty. "You never know!" I told myself. So I decided to take my own advice because deep down I didn't want to let this go.

In my usual diplomatic style, I responded, "It's nice to hear from you. I very much enjoyed our evening together, too. For me, chemistry is the result of spending time with someone and developing a comfort zone and connection with that person over time. I'd therefore be happy to get together again and see where this goes."

Actually, that wasn't true at all. My past relationships had generally gotten started with a strong physical attraction that led to a series of broken hearts. I realized that this might be a much healthier situation, at least a different one, since I wasn't invested in the outcome either way.

Jim and I began to see each other once a week for the next few weeks. Our dates were lengthy, usually involving an outing, such as a concert or a hike, with a meal either before or after each event. We'd spend five or six hours together and talk nonstop about our pasts, families, friends, careers, interests, and outlooks on life. On our third date, we drove to Baltimore and back for a fundraiser for autism, a cause profoundly personal to me. My son, Adam, who was in his early twenties at that time, is on the high-functioning end of the autism spectrum. I was impressed with Jim's acceptance of my circumstances and with his generosity at the event.

Our fourth date took place in Brookside Botanical Gardens, where we walked among the gorgeous spring flowers and picnicked on a blanket, at which time Jim shared with me the entire saga of his wife Cynthia's tragic illness and death. I found myself moved beyond words to learn the details of what he had endured and began to understand more fully just how giving a man Jim was. We also had a lot of fun going dancing together and listening to live rock music, which we both shared a passion for. I began to recognize that despite the differences in our backgrounds, we were more alike than I had initially thought.

The epitome of a typical Jewish girl from Brooklyn, I was the daughter of Holocaust survivors who independently made their way to Palestine, met there, and served in the military during the creation of the State of Israel. My parents married and lived in Israel for about twenty years. My older sister, Evie, and I were born in Israel and immigrated to the United States with our parents when she was six years old and I was one.

Despite being raised in an apartment in New York City, I was completely enveloped in a Jewish bubble. My parents had sent me to a private Jewish elementary school and *yeshivah* (an Orthodox Jewish) high school. I had also spent ten summers in Jewish sleep-away camps in upstate New York, so it was understood that I would marry a Jewish man and raise Jewish children, which I did the first time around. My children were now grown and identified themselves as Jewish. So with the passing of my parents, I finally gave myself permission to consider getting involved with a Gentile.

Jim's background was the total opposite of mine. He was raised as an only child in Pasadena, California, and lived in the same tract home from age two until he finished high school. His father was a lapsed Catholic who turned the religious aspect of Jim's upbringing over to Jim's mother, a Presbyterian who insisted that Jim attend church every Sunday until her untimely death from cancer when Jim was only ten years old. After that, Jim's father, who had gone along with the weekly church routine, dispensed with that practice altogether, much to Jim's relief. As an adult, Jim considered himself part agnostic and had no interest in religion at all.

I began warming up to Jim significantly. Our time together was fun, interesting, and soulful, but I still couldn't tell if Jim had any romantic feelings toward me, since he made no effort to engage in any physical contact whatsoever, not even to take my hand as we crossed the street. In fact, I thought that he might have a stroke when I showed up for our second date and gave him a peck on the cheek as I approached the booth in the restaurant where he had been waiting for me. I pretended not to notice the crimson color he turned and simply acted as if nothing had happened.

For once, the matchmaker, who had always invited feedback after each date she facilitated, was at a loss herself. So, about a month after we met, I offered to bring Chinese food over to the couple who had introduced us so that I could pick their brains about all of this. Deborah, a therapist herself, helped me manage my anxiety around my uncertainty. Her husband, Spence, who knew Jim very well, advised me not to try to take the lead, which was something I would have been very tempted to do. Knowing Jim as he did, he explained that Jim would not invest time with me unless he had a romantic interest in me. He encouraged me to be patient, which has never come naturally to me. He also suggested that I give Jim time and, as the psychiatrist in the room, gently suggested that I work on my impulse to control the dynamic between us. Given what Jim had gone through with the loss of Cynthia, Spence explained that it would make complete sense for Jim to take it slow and play his cards close to the vest.

I was so grateful for their advice. If they hadn't given me their pearls of wisdom, I could have blown things between Jim and me by trying to define or force the situation. Instead, I told myself that I was ready to start taking others' advice and surrender to what the universe might or might not have in store for me.

It only took three more dates for things to become clear. Sitting outside on a beautiful spring evening at a trendy neighborhood restaurant, Jim spontaneously took my hand in his. "Oh," I said. "This is nice. In fact, I have to tell you, I'm not used to this pace of dating. Not that I'm in any rush," I continued, "but I *have* been wondering whether things were going in a particular direction or not." Then I kept quiet.

"They're *going* in a direction, all right," he said. "In fact, I'd love to kiss you tonight." A sense of joy swept over me after hearing these words. "You know by now that I'm not an asshole, right?" he continued. I laughed and nodded. "I just have to say," he paused, "that I didn't see a Jewish girl from Brooklyn in my future."

Without skipping a beat, I shot back, "Well, I didn't see a WASP from Pasadena in mine either!" My response both surprised and tickled him.

"Well, I guess it's on then!" he said.

Jim went on to explain how he had been supercautious about getting involved with anyone if he didn't see a potential future with them. He hadn't been interested in just "getting laid," as many newly single men are prone to do, which explained his apprehension to touch or kiss me. To further clarify, Jim used a musical analogy from when he had made a living as a keyboard player while touring with a band in the early '70s before going back to school to pursue a doctorate in psychology. "During all this time we've spent together," he explained, "I kept looking for a 'false note' but couldn't find it."

I blushed from a mixture of happiness along with a serious wine buzz. "Despite all my issues," I thought, "this man thinks I might be right for him." While I wasn't sure myself, I was open to finding out.

As promised, we kissed in his car in my condo parking lot when he dropped me off. His kiss was gentle and sensuous, yet urgent. I was delighted that he was such a good kisser and excited by the promise of what was yet to come.

I invited Jim upstairs. He paused at my front balcony entrance. As I opened the door, I could see my daughter, Elana, who was living with me temporarily to save money for graduate school, sitting on the living room couch blaring the latest episode of *The Bachelor*, which was one of her favorite guilty pleasures. I wasn't sure what was more embarrassing, the fact that she was home unexpectedly or that my daughter, whom I had described to Jim as ambitious and intelligent, was a fan of that show.

I turned to Jim and told him that we'd have to take a rain check "on the rest" and walked him back down to the car where we continued to kiss for a while longer before I reluctantly broke away to end the evening. Perhaps it was a blessing in disguise, but it didn't feel that way at the time. Actually, the anticipation of being alone together after months of dating without any physical contact sweetened the process. The next time we met, it was clear what was in store. We both acknowledged our nervousness but overcame it quickly with our building passion for one another, which was finally consummated and made even more special by having waited.

I slept surprisingly well after our first night together. When I got up the next morning to make coffee, I returned to the bedroom to find Jim in tears. I panicked. "Maybe this was too soon for him?" I wondered. "Was he crying for his late wife?" Preparing myself for a potential letdown, I put down the coffee mugs, got back into bed, stroked his back, and asked him what was wrong.

"I'm sorry to be so emotional," he said, "but I never thought I'd find this again."

I was so relieved and happy. This was about *me*, not about Cynthia. This wonderful man (and lover as well, as I had discovered!) was letting me know how much our night together had meant to him. His display of emotion touched me deeply and gave me the confidence to trust in our budding romance.

## CHAPTER TWO

# *Shuttle Diplomacy*

*I* began working with Joni, a sixty-five-year-old retired social worker, who hired me after attending a singles' presentation, during which I had spoken about my philosophy on dating and relationships. She felt as if we were on similar wavelengths and thus sought out my services. She had never been married but had been in several unhealthy long-term relationships over the years. Joni eventually sought the advice of a talented therapist, who helped her to understand the reasons she'd been drawn to men who were controlling and unable to provide the nurturing she had lacked as a child.

With my help, Joni was determined to pursue a healthier relationship this time. The first few referrals I provided were to men whom she considered interesting and attractive but chemistry was lacking, so I continued my search on her behalf. I then reached out to Robert, a fellow I had known years back who had been in my network, to inquire as to his status. He informed me that he was still single and very open to meeting any client I'd recommend. I then e-mailed him a photo of Joni along with a description, which included her age, where she lived, her city of origin, occupation, religious and political orientations, hobbies and interests, and the reasons why I thought they might be a good match. Robert wrote back that she "looked cute" and he would be interested in meeting her.

Once I knew Robert was onboard to meet her, I provided Joni with his details as well. When she received my e-mail, she called to inform me that they had already met and had dated about four years earlier. I was surprised that Robert hadn't remembered her but chalked it up to "online dating overload." Joni explained that they had been out several times together, she had liked him very much, and she wasn't sure why things never went anywhere between them. Armed with this information, I went back to Robert to learn more. Once I reminded him of the details of their dates together, it all came back to him. He said that he'd liked her but hadn't been very emotionally available back then, which explained why he didn't pursue Joni beyond those few dates. He assured me that he was in a "much different place" now, having worked with a skilled therapist on his issues, and that if Joni were willing to revisit things between them, he would be open to it as well.

Joni was excited to hear this. She told me that since they last met, she had yet to meet anyone nearly as attractive, intelligent, or as interesting as Robert. Apparently, my instincts about them were correct. I told her that he was now much more motivated to meet someone special after working on himself and perhaps the timing had simply been wrong the last time they had dated.

As per my usual protocol, I asked each of them to review their calendars and provide me with dates when they would be available to meet. I also sent Robert a copy of my guidelines, which recommends that the person I recruit for my client treat on the first date. When he received my e-mail, Robert wrote back explaining that he didn't find the expectation that he pay for the date reasonable and that he avoided women who subscribed to

"outdated and sexist dating practices." He further justified his
position by stating how he'd been exploited in the past by women
whom he had dated. In the end, he had spent too much money, to
no avail, and would never put himself in that situation again.

I tried to assure him that the guidelines had come from *me*, not
Joni, and that I knew her to be a fair person, who was open to
sharing financial responsibilities in a relationship. He told me that
he would only meet her if she agreed to waive the requirement
that he treat. While I didn't think his request would be a healthy
way to begin a renewed interaction between them, I didn't want to
insert my own views into their dynamic, so I posed the question to
Joni directly.

I was not surprised when Joni turned Robert down. She
explained that she considered herself to be a very loving and
giving person, and his request implied a lack of generosity and an
inability to give freely in a relationship. I was disappointed that
their date wouldn't be going forward but understood and actually
agreed with her position completely. I then conveyed her response
to Robert, who was shocked to learn that she wouldn't go out with
him for that reason. I shared Joni's sentiments with him, along with
my disappointment that this wasn't going to work out.

Two days later I received a lengthy e-mail from Robert
expressing deep regret about how he had handled the situation.
He said that he had lost sleep over it and, with the help of his
therapist, had come to understand that Joni had triggered him
by making money an issue between them, which he thought
was a shame. I responded by asking him whether he would be
open to feedback on my part and that if so, I preferred a phone
conversation rather than e-mail. He welcomed my offer, and we
agreed to speak.

Robert and I spent over an hour on the phone, during which
I expressed my view that he had squandered a wonderful
opportunity to reconnect with a very desirable woman and that I

appreciated him taking responsibility for that. He explained why he had gotten so triggered and wondered whether I could let Joni know how sorry he was and ask her whether she would be willing to forgive him and give him another chance.

Once again, I went back to Joni to explain how badly Robert felt and to ask her whether she could see past the incident and go out with him without judgment. Knowing what a kind spirit Joni was, I wasn't surprised when she agreed. This time, I assured her, she could expect him to treat without question, and we chuckled together over the valuable lesson that Robert had apparently learned.

*The value of a trusted friend, coach, or professional matchmaker as a go-between cannot be underestimated.*

Of course, agreeing to see each other again is only the beginning of what might or might not turn out to be a fulfilling dating relationship for Joni and Robert now that they've overcome their first hurdle. This referral was resurrected by my functioning as a trusted confidante and intermediary between them. Without my support, that door would have never been reopened. Just as I received support from my good friends when I first began dating Jim and wasn't sure how to understand him, the value of a trusted friend, coach, or professional matchmaker as a go-between cannot be underestimated.

## CHAPTER THREE

# Puppy Love

*S*tarting my freshman year at the University of Pennsylvania was both exciting and terrifying. While I had grown up in Brooklyn and was used to an urban setting, living on the sprawling campus in West Philadelphia felt very different. I was lucky to be assigned a single dorm room in a part of the campus called The Quad. It was an elegant, old structure housing hundreds of other freshman. My section was referred to as Community House.

Aside from the academic opportunities I had at Penn, I was also eager to meet a guy.

That wasn't hard since, to my good fortune, the ratio of men to women on campus was five to one. It was only a matter of weeks before my first opportunity arose.

First, I met Ben, a Jewish fellow from Westchester County, New York, who lived one flight above me in my dorm. We began a flirtation that intensified over the next few weeks. Before things went any further, I decided to tell him that while I was eager to move forward, I was still a virgin and therefore somewhat nervous about taking that next step. Shocked, he responded,

17

"What? I've never heard of an eighteen-year-old virgin from Brooklyn before!"

I was taken aback and felt shamed by his reaction. I didn't think that being a virgin at that age was a stigma; rather, I saw it as an honor that I would bestow upon someone special. Because he mocked me and made me feel so self-conscious, I concluded that he wasn't "the one."

Next, my childhood friend Robin, who was a grade ahead of me at Penn, introduced me to Gary. Gary was my complete opposite. Raised in a small town in Pennsylvania, he was a tall, slender Irish Catholic fellow. Gary was adorable, with straight, sandy-brown hair; twinkling blue eyes, and a small, turned-up nose. He had an outgoing, gregarious personality, which instantly clicked with mine.

Gary and I began hanging out together among Robin's circle of friends and flirted shamelessly over the next month or so. While I was wary of dating a man who wasn't Jewish, I told myself that we were young and I needn't worry about finding a future husband at that point. I was all about living in the moment.

The morning after our first night together in his dorm room, I confided in him that it had been my first time. I had avoided bringing up the topic beforehand after my experience with Ben. Gary was incredulous. "Really," he said, as we snuggled lovingly. "If that's true, you took to it like a duck to water!" he laughed.

We quickly became inseparable. It was wonderful having a "real" boyfriend for the first time in my life. He was fun, passionate, warm, and loving. We spent almost every night together during that first year, either in my dorm room or his. Our routine consisted of attending classes during the day, having dinner together in the cafeteria in the evening, and then playing pinball with a group of friends in the arcade after dinner.

Gary and I enjoyed our friends but would often retire to his dorm room early to watch *Star Trek* before studying, together or separately, until bedtime. On the weekends, we'd sleep in, explore the city, or catch a movie or live band somewhere. Philly was full of interesting music venues to experience. We spent a lot of time at a popular hangout on campus named Longfellows, where we'd congregate, drinking pitchers of beer until the wee hours of the morning.

Gary was the live wire in our crowd. Once, he drank too much and climbed a lamppost, which he fell off of, hitting the concrete sidewalk headfirst. Panicked, I rushed him to the ER. The doctor at the university hospital marveled that he hadn't split his head open and asked me to keep him up all night to test for signs of a concussion. In keeping with his youthful resilience, Gary was perfectly fine the next day.

Life with Gary was a hoot. His personality was larger than life, and I found myself swept up by his energy and enthusiasm. He had a part-time campus job running the student snack program and had a key to the warehouse, which contained all the Hostess snacks that were sold on campus. We spent many nights munching out in that warehouse, which greatly accounted for the "freshman fifteen" I put on that year. Gary also belonged to a long-respected acting and singing troupe called Mask & Wig, which was a Penn institution. He'd have rehearsals late at night and would let himself into my room and bed at about 1:00 a.m., which I sleepily welcomed. He performed with Mask & Wig around the country over Christmas break. When they did a show in Manhattan, I attended and crashed with him in his room at the Plaza Hotel. We had a blast, despite the fact that we had to share the room with two fellow performers.

In the spring semester, we enrolled in Introduction to Sociology together, thinking we'd inspire each other. Instead, we distracted each other to the point where I almost flunked my midterm exam. Afterward, Gary and I decided that taking classes together wasn't the best idea.

When the weather got warmer, Gary and I decided to go camping on the spur of the moment with some equipment we had collected from a few different friends. We hitchhiked to a nearby campground and warmed some hot dogs and beans over the campfire for dinner that night. The sound effects emanating from the double sleeping bag that we had borrowed had us cracking up the entire night.

I was the happiest I had ever been, until it all came crashing down toward the end of the spring semester. One night, we assembled in my friend Kathy's off-campus apartment, and I began to feel sick. Kathy suggested that I sleep over rather than walk back to my dorm. Gary insisted on staying behind to make sure I'd be okay. When I woke up the next day, however, he was gone. Linda, one of Kathy's roommates, turned beat red and averted her eyes when she passed me in the hallway. She had had a crush on Gary the entire year, so I immediately knew something was wrong and confronted Kathy about it. As my good friend, she couldn't lie to me and reluctantly told me that Gary and Linda had slept together the previous night. I was devastated. How could my sweetie betray me with a mutual friend in the next room, where I was sick no less?

My heartache was deep and unrelenting. I could barely function through the rest of the semester. I couldn't comprehend how Gary, who I thought loved me, had hurt me so badly. I thought we were happy. What did Linda offer him that I did not? My insecurities took over. I began to blame myself for not being good enough for Gary. I sobbed into my pillow night after night, which could be heard by my next-door neighbor and residential advisor, Duncan. Duncan tried to comfort me, but I was inconsolable.

When the semester ended, I went back to my parents' house in Brooklyn for the summer. My parents had never seen me so unglued. My mother, who was my confidante and emotional safe haven, was shaken to the core by my grief. She cried her eyes out day after day in solidarity with me. She hated Gary for hurting me and would say things like "He took all the joy of life out of you," which didn't help at all and made me feel responsible for her unhappiness as well as my own. Now I had two broken hearts on my hands.

Slowly, I began to come back to my old self. I had several jobs that summer, one of which was working in a nursing home as an administrative assistant. I developed wonderful relationships with some of the residents, who would often come by my desk and regale me with their life stories. They told me about the loves of their lives, their children, their losses, etc. I quickly learned that listening with an open heart, to help support other people emotionally, worked like a tonic to strengthen and heal my own psyche.

Gradually, my grief subsided and transitioned to anger. I obsessed over the way Gary had treated me so shabbily, especially after we had been so close. To make matters worse, according to Kathy, Gary and Linda began sleeping together regularly after that fateful night through the end of the semester until we all left for the summer. She told me that while Linda may have met Gary's sexual needs, it was clear he missed me and simply relied on Linda to fill the void. That provided little comfort, given my demons of rejection and jealousy. I began to fantasize about getting back together with him and then dumping him as cruelly as he had treated me. I vowed I would get even with him somehow when I returned to school in the fall.

Given what had happened, I dreaded going back to Penn for my sophomore year and facing Gary and the gang. I also didn't know how I'd deal with my nemesis, Linda. I resolved not to let Gary or the others see how badly I'd been hurt. Luckily, Gary moved off campus, which reduced my chances of running into him. Kathy and Linda's living situation changed as well. Now that they were no longer roommates, it would be easier for me to spend time with Kathy.

That fall, when Gary and I met again for the first time, I could feel the same magnetic pull between us, despite everything that had happened. I could see the pain in his eyes behind his usual boyish grin. It was bittersweet to be around each other. We both clearly missed each other and felt a huge void after spending nearly every day together the previous year.

I plunged into my studies and started making new friends. Gary and I continued to find ourselves together in various social situations, however. The energy between us was palpable and obvious to our friends. The first time Gary and I ran into each other on campus, he asked if we could talk. I agreed. We sat under an old familiar oak tree on Locust Walk, the main artery that ran through campus.

"I want you to know that I still love you," he began, "and not a day goes by that I haven't kicked myself for what I did to you." My eyes welled with tears. These were the words I'd been dying to hear. "I wouldn't blame you if you tell me to fuck off," he continued, "but if you can find it in your heart to forgive me and give me another chance, it would mean everything to me. We had a great thing going, and I stupidly blew it for a silly flirtation with someone I wasn't in love with. I'm so sorry I hurt you."

By then, I was crying quietly, tears streaming down my face. Could I trust him again? I wasn't sure. I had missed him terribly, but could we really pick up where we left off? He could see how moved and conflicted I was.

"This is a lot for me to take in," I said. "I'll need some time to digest this and to think about it," I replied. Really, all I wanted to do was to fall into his arms as I had done so many times before.

My wounded pride prevented me from giving in so quickly; I thought he should at least stew for a while in my indecision. It felt empowering for me to take back the control in our relationship. He agreed to give me all the space I needed. A few weeks later, I decided to give him another chance. My friends already assumed it was a done deal, so my announcement that we were back together came as no surprise to anyone.

Our routines were different this time. Since Gary lived off campus, it took more of an effort for us to get together, and we didn't automatically sleep together every night. I developed more of my own social life without him and his circle of friends. While I still cherished my time with Gary, it felt like part of the magic between us had disappeared, which was understandable given the wounds I was still trying to heal from. I couldn't completely snuff out the doubts that lurked in the back of my mind.

Between the time I spent with Gary and my newfound social life, the year passed rather quickly. I decided that law was my calling and chose political science as my major and psychology as my minor. I had received a work-study grant for a full-time summer position and found a fabulous job working for the Philadelphia district attorney's office in their newly established Domestic Violence Unit. The thought of going back to my parents' house in Brooklyn wasn't particularly appealing after the depressing summer I'd spent with them the year before. Gary told me that his lease was good through late August and he had decided to stay in Philly and work full time that summer. He invited me to live with him and his roommate, Peter, in their two bedroom, off-campus apartment. I wasn't sure whether this was a good idea or not, but it made practical sense. Also, I thought that living together would be a good test for the future of our relationship.

In the summer of 1977, I moved in with him in his three-story, walk-up apartment with no air conditioning. I found working full time and then returning to his apartment in the heat of the summer to be completely oppressive. The only relief was to shower every few hours. Naturally, our sex life suffered as a result of the physical discomfort we were in. More and more, I looked forward to leaving in the morning for the air-conditioned office I worked in. The work was quite compelling, and I often stayed there after hours. In keeping with my passion for helping domestic violence victims, I volunteered to spend my Saturday nights filing emergency protection orders in the police administration building downtown.

Gary and I slowly grew apart that summer. He worked as
a bartender at a high-end restaurant in the evenings, so our
schedules barely coincided. We became "ships in the night" in
terms of our schedules, and my attention began to wander from
Gary. I found myself attracted to other men whom I met through
my job. One weekend, a very cute, young lawyer, whom I worked
with at the police building, asked me out for a drink. I accepted.
Even though I told him that I had a boyfriend right away and he
was respectful of my boundaries, I wondered what it would be like
to date him.

By the end of the summer, I decided that my relationship with
Gary had run its course. Oddly enough, the thing I had wished
for the most came true. I felt no feelings of triumph over this
imminent breakup, just sadness that it had not worked out. When
I informed Gary that I thought we should end it, he took it hard.
I was surprised that he hadn't felt the same sense of estrangement
that I had and wanted things to continue. It felt anticlimactic. My
fantasy of breaking his heart as payback for mine turned out to be
an empty victory from which I derived no vindication or pleasure.

## CHAPTER FOUR

# The Bloom Falls Off the Rose

*C*onnie and Randall were a couple in their fifties whom I had introduced to each other in December 2002. They liked each other and began dating exclusively right out of the starting gate. I was delighted that I had hit a "home run" on my first referral for Randall. He was a scientist working for a federal agency who'd never been married; she was self-employed and a single mom of two children, whom Connie introduced to Randall about three months into their relationship. Randall got along very well with Connie's kids and soon became a regular presence during Connie's weekends with them.

It was a happy time for them. Connie, who'd been through a bad divorce two years earlier, began to relax into their relationship and started to envision a future with Randall, who craved a family connection, given that he had little to no family himself. Randall was generous and sweet, always treating Connie and the kids whenever they were together.

That spring Connie and Randall drove to Woodstock, New York, to meet some friends of Connie's from LA who were there to attend a family wedding. This would be their first time on an extended road trip and weekend together. They drove in Randall's new Mercedes, since he wanted a chance to try the car out on a long drive. During their seven-hour journey, they listened to their favorite music and happily chatted the entire time. When they finally arrived in the town of Woodstock, Randall deftly squeezed into a parking spot on Main Street.

Connie and Randall had a wonderful evening over dinner with Connie's friends at a trendy restaurant nearby. Afterward, they returned to the car to drive to a small bed and breakfast they had booked about a mile down the road. Just as they got into their car, the car in front of them backed into Randall's fender as the driver tried to maneuver out of the tight parking spot. Randall became irate, got out of the car, and began cursing at the driver just as he began apologizing profusely for tapping Randall's fender, which didn't even leave a scratch. Connie was taken aback at Randall's fury, especially since the incident didn't even damage his car. Randall, on the other hand, was unforgiving and nasty to the other driver, insisting that he take down his information in the event any problems arose with his precious new Mercedes.

Connie got very upset about how Randall had handled himself in that situation and told him as much, which put a damper on the rest of their weekend. This was the first clue that Randall had a problem with anger, which Connie hadn't discerned before. Eventually, they moved beyond the incident and their relationship continued through the summer. On the Fourth of July, they decided to drive to New York City to visit Connie's brother and sister-in-law in Manhattan, who would be meeting Randall for the first time. Their plan was to use Connie's brother's friend's penthouse apartment at Waterside, a high-rise overlooking the East River, to view the fireworks. They were excited to have one of the best views in the city for the event.

The initial introductions between Randall and Connie's family went well. They went out to a festive dinner, where Connie could discern that her brother and sister-in-law "approved" of Randall and were enjoying his company. After dinner, they made their way over to Waterside, which was packed with throngs of spectators waiting for the fireworks to start. It took a good half hour for them to make their way through the crowd, into the building, and up the elevator to the penthouse. When they finally got to the apartment door and tried the keys, to their tremendous frustration, they discovered that the keys didn't work. Connie's sister-in-law immediately called the friend who owned the apartment for help and, as it turned out, to their embarrassment, the friend had left them the wrong keys. It also became clear that, due to the crowds, the doorman was not available to help them gain access. Thus, they needed to make other plans. Suddenly, Randall threw a major tantrum and began stamping his foot and yelling about their friend's stupidity in making such a bad mistake. Connie was mortified.

Needless to say, Connie's family's impression of Randall took a nose dive. Connie began to question the relationship herself. After much soul searching, she decided to break up with him. She was sad to lose him, but she reassured herself that it was the right decision. She didn't need a man in her life who was prone to outbursts at such an early stage in their relationship. "Just imagine how it would be if we lived together or married," she reasoned.

The following holiday season, Connie ran into Randall at a holiday party. Neither of them had met anyone else since their breakup, and seeing each other rekindled the feelings between them. The following day, Connie wrote Randall an e-mail expressing her continued love for him and her regret over the way things had ended so abruptly between them. She said she missed him terribly and pleaded with him to consider getting back together. Randall was touched by this and felt he couldn't walk away from the strength of her feelings toward him. They talked through what had happened and Randall took full responsibility for his behavior and resolved to work on his anger issues so they could move forward on a healthier basis.

The pair resumed their relationship, which was still passionate as well as comforting to them both. Months later, however, it seemed as if the magic had washed out of their relationship. Connie felt like she was waiting for "the other shoe to drop" every time something didn't go smoothly between them; Randall felt as if he couldn't shake the cloud of judgment hanging over his head, despite Connie's assurances that she had forgiven him. They both began to feel as if they were "going through the motions" in their relationship and eventually came to the mutual conclusion that it was best for them to move on. They acknowledged that they had tried, but given the breech they had experienced at such an early stage in their relationship, they just couldn't move beyond it successfully.

## CHAPTER FIVE

# Swiss Indulgence

Claud stood out at Penn. He was strikingly handsome with long, layered silky brown hair and piercing green eyes. He had an air of quiet dignity about him, bordering on arrogance. He'd registered as a transfer student from Switzerland, where his American parents had raised him from the age of three.

Claud's family had led a very exclusive life living in a mountaintop villa in a small town in the Swiss Alps. His father owned a very successful international insurance business that took him all over the world. As such, Claud had led a privileged life, attending a prestigious boarding school in the United States for high school. Afterward, he enrolled at Penn for his freshman year but was suddenly called back to Switzerland for a family crisis brought on by his father's business tanking. Claud's father had no other option but to declare bankruptcy, which is a crime in Switzerland. Authorities immediately took him into custody, and Claud flew back to Switzerland to help his mother pack up their house. He returned to the United States with his mother, with nothing more than a trunk full of clothes to her name, out of fear of her being arrested.

After a year's leave of absence, Claud returned to Penn. His mother, Margaret, who had grown up in Michigan, was a high achiever herself. Thus, she was determined to help Claud get through school. She rented a tenement apartment downtown and, at age sixty-two, got a job as a secretary for a professional association within walking distance of their apartment.

Claud's transition from "riches to rags" was very tough on him. I had known him the prior year and had been somewhat put off by his air of superiority. When he reappeared on campus after his circumstances had changed, his energy felt entirely different. He seemed humbled and grateful to be back.

Always popular with women, Claud was actually quite shy once you got to know him, as I later discovered. One evening in late October, we found ourselves at the same Halloween party. I came dressed as a high-class call girl in a costume that showcased my size 4 figure at the time. Dressed in a sheik's outfit, he definitely noticed me as well. After an evening of partying and flirtation, I invited him back to my apartment, where we spent the night together. It was surprisingly passionate and sweet. I told myself that this was just a fling and nothing serious would come of it. I didn't really know whether or not I even liked him. We made no promises to each other after that night but continued to hook up on a regular basis.

Over time, without planning or realizing it, Claud and I fell in love. This became obvious one Friday evening during a walk at sunset when we found ourselves sitting on the famous steps of the Philadelphia Art Museum, where the movie *Rocky* was filmed. Without the possibility of anything going further, we held hands and kissed for a long time. Then we looked at each other, grinned, and hugged a bit longer.

I began spending nights with Claud and Margaret in their downtown apartment. She welcomed any girlfriend of Claud's, given her liberal views on sex and the social isolation she struggled with. Claud eventually opened up about his conflicts with his narcissistic father and his empathy for his mother. Margaret also confided in me about the suffering she had endured in her marriage due to her husband's constant travels and various indiscretions, which she was fully aware of. She treated me like a member of their family and related to me as if I were the daughter she wished she'd had.

Claud wasn't Jewish, so my own mother wasn't too thrilled about this relationship. I had also become so close to Margaret that my mother felt threatened and somewhat envious of my connection to her at that time. I tried to reassure her that no one could replace her, but my mother's obvious judgment of my relationship placed an inevitable distance between us. My father, on the other hand, was left completely in the dark.

Having Claud as a boyfriend was interesting. Women envied me for being with such a fantastic looking guy. I often wondered whether they asked themselves what he was doing with me. I was still plagued by my own insecurities about my looks, which were decent but, in my opinion, didn't measure up to his. Claud, however, thought I was pretty and incredibly sexy, and he loved me wholeheartedly. He was completely loyal and never gave me any reason to worry about other women. We also encouraged each other academically, such as with his interest in transferring to Wharton to study business and my plans to apply to law school.

That spring, Claud and Margaret's landlord suddenly evicted them from their building, which would be torn down. Presuming they had no resources to fight him, their landlord, an unscrupulous slumlord, refused to return their security deposit. To Margaret, that money was a fortune.

I was outraged at how their landlord had treated them and went on a crusade to get their money back. I still worked as an intern in the DA's office at the time and researched the landlord's identity and contact information. I called him, explained that I worked at the DA's office, and demanded that he return their security deposit. Frightened by my call, he said that he "didn't want any trouble" and agreed to send them a check. I was delighted and proclaimed to my supervisor that I "had won my first case." When I explained the details to her, she was not impressed and warned me to be very careful about "stepping over my skis." My disappointment at her reaction receded, however, when Margaret received her check. She couldn't have been happier and more grateful.

I felt like I had done a wonderful thing until I learned that my call to the landlord almost got me fired. He was a very powerful, local real estate developer who knew one of the assistant DAs. He called him to inquire about me, but incredibly, out of over one hundred assistants at the DA's office, the landlord happened to call the one whom I had become friends with. He knew me, knew all about my situation with Claud, and was kind enough to vouch for my character. He pleaded with the landlord not to pursue this any further with the "big boss," the district attorney. The landlord accused me of misrepresenting myself as an attorney, when I was simply a college intern. In truth, he had only inferred that I was an attorney when I stated that I worked at the DA's office. My friend assured him that I hadn't intended to commit fraud and persuaded him to drop his vendetta against me. While I dodged a major bullet in my zeal to help Margaret and Claud, I admit that I got a secret thrill out of intimidating such a powerful man. As a result, Claud and Margaret moved into a nicer, but still modest, apartment on Spruce Street, where we continued to function as a family.

The following Christmas, Claud's father flew in from London, where he had been living since his release from prison. Margaret and Claud insisted that I join them for dinner at a very ritzy restaurant, which was his father's style. I reluctantly agreed, since I was curious after everything I'd heard about him.

William showed up larger than life. A tall, handsome, older gentleman, he carried a box with a new and rather large color

TV for their new apartment under one arm and designer luggage laden with gifts under the other. Dinner itself was opulent and awkward. The shock on his face was obvious once he saw how Margaret and Claud were living. Oddly enough, he never said a word about it. He didn't appear thrilled to see me in the picture either. I wasn't sure whether this was because of my Jewish heritage or perhaps because he felt like I wasn't beautiful enough for Claud. Either way, I was proud of how Margaret and Claud introduced me as Claud's girlfriend and wanted me along.

Still legally married, Margaret and her husband had been separated for several years. I wondered whether he'd stay at the Ritz or the Four Seasons. To my surprise, Margaret invited him to stay with them. She even allowed him into her bed after everything that had taken place between them. I told myself that this was none of my business, but I couldn't help feeling that Margaret demeaned herself somehow by sharing her bed with a husband who had treated her so shabbily. "Clearly, she still has feelings for him, in spite of everything," I thought.

I felt guilty for judging her. After all, she had put up with Claud and me sleeping in the next room together and must have heard the sounds of our own lovemaking over the music she played in her room. "Maybe some physical pleasure would be a nice thing for her to experience after going without for so long," I reasoned, "even from a man so unworthy."

Claud and I had been together for a year and a half when I got accepted into law school at Hofstra University in New York. He had also achieved his goal of transferring to Wharton, but given the leave of absence he'd taken, he was a grade behind me. This was the first acceptance letter I had received, and I had no choice but to give them an answer before I heard back from the other schools that I had applied to. Since I didn't know whether or not I'd get accepted anywhere else, I agonized over the decision and was reluctant to roll the dice in case I didn't. Accepting Hofstra's offer meant moving to the Long Island suburbs, leaving Claud and Margaret, and starting a new life. Despite this, I had worked so hard to get into law school and didn't want to take any risks; therefore, I reluctantly accepted.

Hofstra had a great law program, and Claud and I had talked many times about trying to keep our relationship going, despite the upcoming distance between us. In the back of my mind, I remembered the photo of Nella, Claud's former girlfriend in Switzerland, which stood at his bedside when we first began our afternoon interludes. It seemed so long ago. Eventually, that photo disappeared, and he never spoke of it. "Would that be my fate?" I wondered.

Claud and I tried to make the most of our time together before my departure, but my sadness over our impending separation clouded everything. The lump in my throat persisted through my graduation day, which should have been a happy event. Instead, it was heartbreaking. My parents attended and, while they took great pride in my achievement, they were terribly saddened by the emotional pain I was in.

That summer, my mother, who owned a travel agency in Manhattan, gifted me a fabulous trip through Europe and Israel. Claud had secured an amazing internship in Lagos, Nigeria, through some of his father's connections. To help ease the pain of his absence, I made it a point to travel to Claud's hometown in Switzerland, where Claud had arranged for me to stay with his childhood friends. They hosted me warmly and generously.

I was on an odyssey to connect with Claud's past as I pined for him. I had seen photos of where he grew up but, once there, I was blown away by its beauty. The town looked like a movie set, complete with snow covered mountains, wooden chalets filled with flowered window boxes, and cows grazing lazily to the sound of cowbells in the crisp mountain air. I hiked to Claud's childhood home, which was perched on the side of a mountain. It had been sold when the family fled the country. I sat across from the house envisioning their young family and sobbing for his loss, as well as for mine.

The following fall, I began my first year of law school. It was every bit as stressful as people had warned me. I felt overwhelmed with having to adjust to living with strangers in university housing and absorbing hundreds of pages of law textbooks, which my professors expected me to master. Plus, I missed Claud desperately.

On the first holiday weekend, Claud traveled from Philly to visit. It was a wonderful reunion, despite my living situation. At the end of the weekend, I asked him where he thought our relationship was headed. He told me that he loved me and wanted it to continue. I felt insecure about the distance and wanted more of a commitment from him. He reluctantly offered the option of marriage. This was hardly the romantic proposal I had envisioned, but I was thrilled that he initiated the idea and readily agreed to be informally engaged.

Over the next few days, however, my happiness was short-lived; our agreement didn't sit well with me. I called Claud, and he expressed the same feelings. It felt rushed and ill-advised to us both. I was dismayed to hear he'd been feeling nauseous since the weekend, which was a bad sign. We were both relieved that we felt the same way and agreed to continue the relationship without the pressure of an engagement. Given where we were in our lives, neither one of us was in any position to plan or to afford to commit to anything long-term. Nonetheless, I felt deflated by this setback and wondered what would become of us. Later that fall, I visited him in Philly and could feel that things had changed. He didn't seem quite as enthusiastic to see me and made less of an effort to accommodate me by making excuses not to meet me or take me back to the train station.

An interesting experience occurred that Christmas. Since the beginning of the semester, the university dorm where I lived was undergoing renovations to partition each unit and turn the common space into a second bedroom. I welcomed this project, since I had been living in the apartment living room and had craved my privacy.

I became friendly with a fellow named George, who was one of the contractors on the project. He was a tall, dark, curly haired, and buff fellow in his thirties who filled in his overalls impressively. Perhaps it was my Brooklyn roots, but I'd always had a thing for men in overalls, having passed a construction site or two growing up. I'd greet him every morning on my way to the elevator in my building. We'd chit chat on occasion, which always cheered me up, and he was kind enough to give my apartment priority on the list of units to be renovated after I had bemoaned my lack of privacy. To my disappointment, he disappeared once he completed the work, and I began to wonder where he had gone.

> **I do want to give you two words of advice: First, never settle. Second, don't become hard.**

In late December, the building hosted a Christmas party. Suddenly, there he stood looking fabulous in his tight jeans and collared shirt. He spied me from across the room and walked over. I immediately noticed that he'd been drinking.

"Merry Christmas, George," I said. "It's nice to see you again."

He looked me straight in the eye and said, "I didn't walk over to you to ask for your number. In fact, you'll never see me again after tonight. I came over to deliver a message."

"Okay," I said tentatively and quietly listened.

"I've been observing you," he continued, "and I can tell that you're a woman who knows herself and knows what she wants. I can also tell you've been through some things. I don't need to know the details, but I do want to give you two words of advice:

First, never settle. Second, don't become hard. Too many women walk around with chips on their shoulders, and it's impossible for men to get close to them. If you stick to these two principles in life, you'll do all right." Then he turned on his heels and disappeared across the room into the crowd.

I'd had a drink or two myself and was touched by that sweet and profound interaction. True to his word, I never saw or heard from him again. I actually called the building administrator to inquire of his whereabouts, but they couldn't give me any information. He had simply vanished, as promised. I gave much thought to his simple words of advice, which have stuck with me ever since, and which I've tried my best to live by. To this day, I believe that George was my angel in overalls.

After the holidays, I moved out of university housing into a group home within walking distance of the law school. There, I had my own room and a semiprivate entrance. My roommates were wonderful. They were all guys, but two of them had serious girlfriends who spent a lot of time in the house with us as well. One of the guys was a gourmet chef and loved to cook for us all. We were lucky to have him cook house dinners for us on most weeknights. This led to a wonderful feeling of camaraderie between us. I was especially close to Larry, an adorable red-headed fellow from Philly. He took a personal interest in my well-being, despite having a serious girlfriend. I was relieved that she was completely cool with our friendship.

Claud came to visit me that spring and was, by necessity, subject to my roommates' scrutiny. I found him to be even more emotionally distant and embarrassingly curt with my roommates, who'd heard so much about him. We had an awkward weekend together in the house, and they reluctantly gave me a "thumbs down" review of him after he left. I was hurt and defensive but, in my heart, agreed with their assessment, although I kept clinging to hope that the old Claud would somehow re-emerge. George's

words of wisdom circled around my brain. "Don't settle," he had
said. Was my continuing the relationship settling? I asked myself.

In May, I was forced to buckle down for finals and cram what
I could into a few weeks of intensive study. The night before my
Contracts exam, I got a call from Peter, my ex-boyfriend Gary's
old roommate from Penn, who was now a graduate student there
and who had remained a good friend, even after my breakup with
Gary. We spent some time catching up, and then he informed
me that he'd run into Claud and his new girlfriend, Judith. I
was stunned. "Judith who?" I asked. Peter quickly realized he'd
overstepped by saying anything. I couldn't help pumping him for
information and learned that Claud had begun seeing a physician
named Judith, who was considerably older than he was. I was
devastated. Poor Peter felt terrible to be the one to inadvertently
break the news to me. I thanked him for his honesty and ended the
call while I still had my dignity intact. Then I broke down.

The next day, I sat for my Contracts exam in a state of shock
and barely passed. I was a zombie for the next few weeks, unable
to sleep or to fully absorb anything I studied. My grades reflected
this, and I was placed on academic probation. I was determined to
turn things around after the summer, however, when I returned for
my second year.

Meanwhile, Claud graduated from Wharton. He invited me
to attend, but I declined. I was way too hurt and wondered if
he'd bring Judith instead. After all, he could show off the fact
that he had an older, professional woman on his arm. Later,
he called to let me know he'd gotten a job in Manhattan at
a commodities firm and would be renting an apartment in
Brooklyn, close to my parents' home, where I'd be spending
the summer. He then invited me to come see him at his new
apartment nearby. My response was cold and unwelcoming,
which took him aback. It took all my strength to end the call
quickly. I knew how dangerous it would be for me to open that

door again. With all the will I could muster, I politely declined and simply wished him well.

That summer, while I was still recovering from my breakup with Claud, an Israeli fellow a few years older than me named Ari arrived on my parents' doorstep. He was the nephew of my mother's old friend from Israel. He had come to New York to study stage design. My parents quickly took to him, almost like the son they'd never had, and rented their downstairs studio apartment to him. When I met him, I was struck by the fact that with his reddish curly hair, he could have easily passed for my brother. Later, we joked that perhaps we were really siblings and no one had told us. He was incredibly smart, talented, and funny, and he had the "Israeli macho" thing going for him. I was hardly in the mood to embrace a new person in my life, but gradually, we became friends, and I shared my Claud saga with him. He listened carefully and then said in Hebrew, "I swear to God, if you even think of going near him again, I'll break both his legs!" I was shocked by his aggression but also touched by his protectiveness. I didn't doubt for a minute that he'd follow through on this threat, so I heeded his warning and stayed away from Claud, something I'll always be grateful to Ari for.

## CHAPTER SIX

# All That Glitters

An affiliate matchmaker in New York referred Jackie to me as a match for one of my male clients who was searching for an exceedingly beautiful and classy Jewish woman in her early fifties. When I initially vetted Jackie on Daniel's behalf, it was clear to me that she was a woman of quality who had her own high standards for the men she considered dating. I was impressed with Jackie and decided to give this match a try but, of course, wasn't sure whether or not the physical chemistry would be there between them, as is the big "wild card" in every referral.

Daniel and Jackie met, but, unfortunately, there were absolutely no sparks between them. While that was a disappointing outcome for Daniel, Jackie and I had such a positive interaction between us that she asked me to represent her in her own search for a life partner. She explained that she had already met so many prospects in her area that she felt it would be more productive to widen her search and hire a matchmaker in the DC area, where both her daughters lived and where she therefore spent a lot of time and could contemplate relocating to, for the right man.

Jackie's first referral was pleasant, but neither of them felt attracted enough to the other to warrant a second date. Based on feedback from both of them, I proposed that Pablo be her next referral. Pablo was a tall, handsome, Jewish man who had been raised in Buenos Aires. His Latin and Jewish roots made for a rather interesting combination. Fifty-eight at the time, Pablo had immigrated to the United States in his early thirties while married to the mother of his two children. He was an entrepreneur who traveled frequently on business as well as to compete in tango competitions around the world. I predicted that Jackie would be strongly attracted to such a graceful and sophisticated man.

When Pablo and I first discussed the idea of him meeting Jackie, I explained that she lived in New York and inquired as to whether he would be open to a long-distance situation, hopefully leading to a serious, permanent relationship. I let him know that Jackie would be prepared to move to the DC area if things were to become serious between them. He assured me he was seriously searching for his next wife and that given his frequent business trips to New York, he could easily accommodate such an arrangement. Given those assurances, I introduced them to each other, and, as I had predicted, Jackie was indeed taken with Pablo, as he was with her.

Singing Pablo's praises, Jackie called me on the way home from their first date and thanked me for introducing her to such a unique man. She told me how Pablo immediately suggested ways in which the two of them could meet up, either in New York or DC or somewhere in between, in order for them to spend as much time together as possible. The following morning, Pablo enthusiastically texted me to let me know that he really liked Jackie as well and I had done a wonderful job.

They subsequently got into an intense texting pattern, which was actually contrary to my advice. Pablo would text her almost every hour of every day to let her know how his days were going and to pile on the compliments, so Jackie felt like they were "an item" before they even had a second date. Jackie was excited and flattered by Pablo's constant attention and hopeful that they'd spend parts of the upcoming holiday season together.

Meanwhile, Jackie took a long-planned trip to Europe with a friend. She felt frustrated that she wouldn't have a chance to see Pablo until afterward, but he assured her before her departure that he'd keep in touch and would make plans to meet her as soon as she got back. True to his word, he texted her twice daily at a minimum, and she responded regularly, taking the time difference into account. Via text, they arranged for him to drive up to New York on the weekend following her return. She agreed to meet him in Manhattan so that he could shave a few hours off his drive. Pablo told her that he couldn't wait to see her again and was counting the days until her return.

On the night of their date, a storm system rolled in and dropped buckets of rain, sleet, and hail up and down the Eastern seaboard. Pablo had reserved a hotel room at the Hyatt near Grand Central Station so he could take a train back and forth from DC. They met in the hotel lobby and decided to eat in the hotel restaurant, given the terrible weather, which got increasingly worse as the evening progressed. Their time together was romantic, flirty, and fun, but Jackie became more concerned about driving back to Long Island the later it got. Pablo offered to share his room with her "for safety reasons" so she didn't risk driving home in such dangerous conditions. She agreed that his suggestion made the most sense.

The following day, Jackie called to report in after her date. She informed me that she had stayed over in Pablo's room due to the weather. I wondered to myself why she didn't get her own room, especially since it was so early in their developing relationship and she could well afford it.

As she explained it, the evening was "somewhat romantic," but they chose to refrain from actually having sex with each other.

While I wasn't sure what she meant, I was reluctant to press further for the details. Suffice it to say, she felt closer to him as a result of that experience and was under the impression that his feelings for her remained as strong as ever. At breakfast, however, when she proposed that it was her turn to travel to him and attempted to pin down a date that would work for both their schedules, he equivocated and refused to commit to a specific date, explaining that he had to check his schedule with his kids.

Shortly thereafter, his hourly text messages stopped. Jackie sensed that she was about to be "ghosted" by him. She was hurt and angry at the fact that he appeared to have dropped her like a hot potato, and she refused to reach out to him to see what was going on.

Pablo was unresponsive to my initial efforts to reach him to get his direct feedback. In my discussions with Jackie about what had transpired, I ventured a theory that perhaps he had gotten frustrated with what had occurred in their hotel room and decided to drop the whole thing. She disagreed, saying that she thought he was a "total player" and that he had been using her like a "truck stop" in his travels, even though they had never consummated their relationship. She also suspected that he had someone local and that he had been using her the entire time, refusing to consider any other point of view.

I finally heard back from Pablo, who explained that he had come to the realization that a long-distance dating situation wasn't going to work for him because his schedule had gotten significantly busier since their initial introduction. His explanation didn't quite add up in my mind, as he knew full well going into it that the commitment would involve distance. I asked him point-blank whether he was seeing someone else locally. He credibly denied it, repeating his assertion that he just came to the conclusion that the situation would be too stressful to maintain. He claimed that he didn't want to raise expectations on Jackie's part that he was unable to fulfill, so he thought it best to cut it off earlier rather than later.

That explanation, while understandable on one level, gave me pause. Something had made him suddenly cool off to Jackie. Perhaps Jackie was right about him. I surmised that Pablo had hoped for sex the night he and Jackie stayed in his hotel room together, and when it hadn't quite happened that way, Pablo decided it wasn't worth the effort. Poor Jackie. She really liked him and was crushed at what had happened. But then again, if she had had sex with him that night and he had still dropped her unceremoniously, it might have been so much worse for her. I found myself wishing that she had played her cards differently with him, but I will never know what he really felt in his heart.

## CHAPTER SEVEN

# True Love Sacrificed

*R*aised in Leipzig, Germany, my mother was the eldest of four children and the only redhead in a family of brunettes. Like many redheads, she was quite passionate and had an iron will, all four feet eleven of her. Active in the Zionist movement in Germany, she requested permission from her parents to leave Germany, unaccompanied, for what was then Palestine, at just sixteen years old, to support the establishment of the State of Israel. She would then join up with her peers from other countries to settle on a *kibbutz*, or farm collective. Justifiably concerned with the entire family's survival under Nazi Germany, my grandparents reluctantly agreed.

In 1938, my grandparents accompanied my mother to the central train station in Leipzig, the largest train station in Europe. They said their goodbyes not knowing whether or not they would ever see one another again. Bound for Italy, my mother would later board a ship and join other youth who were being smuggled into Palestine.

My mother wasn't the first to make the trip. My grandparents sent my mother's younger brother, Lothar, to London at age fifteen. My grandfather had connections in the fur industry there, and in order to ensure my uncle's safety, he arranged for him to work in London as an apprentice. Uncle Lothar remained in London until his death at age ninety-three.

My mother's first cousins, Benno and Hertel, were sent by their parents to England on the Kindertransport to ensure their survival as well. Just teenagers at the time, they settled in Gwrych Castle in Wales with about forty other refugees under the auspices of the Jewish Orthodox movement in England. They fully expected to be reunited with their families eventually, but, tragically, that never came to pass. They remained together as a group until each of them turned eighteen and made their way to London to begin their lives anew.

The rest of the family, including my grandparents and my mother's two younger sisters, remained in Leipzig. Just six months after my mother departed Germany, authorities deported the family to Krakow, Poland, from where they were eventually transported to a concentration camp, which we believe to have been Auschwitz. There they eventually perished.

My mother arrived in Palestine and was assigned to a kibbutz, where she lived for two years before being eligible for army service. She, along with her peers, joined the British army, which occupied Palestine at the time. Assigned to a Jewish battalion, she served in Egypt for several years.

After the war, my mother made her way to Haifa, where she had an aunt who had arrived in Israel from Munich years earlier. My mother took odd jobs to support herself and enrolled in nursing school. While in Haifa, she met my father, a naval security officer, while attempting to enter a military base with a jeep full of army nurses.

She had been stopped at the security checkpoint because she lacked proper identification. My father, who looked quite handsome and impressive in his police uniform, according to my mother, took one look at the striking redhead and told his subordinates not to mess with the *jinjeet* (Hebrew slang for redhead) and to let her pass. Their relationship started from there, culminating in their marriage in 1946, two years before the birth of the State of Israel, which they were privileged to be a part of.

My father was from a small town outside Warsaw, Poland. He had made his way to then Palestine with the Polish army after being imprisoned in a work camp for over two years. My father went AWOL from the Polish army and joined Israeli security forces in Haifa at the urging of a cousin he was able to connect with there. Like my mother's family, his parents and four brothers had perished in the Holocaust as well.

My parents bore witness to the creation of the State of Israel. This, along with their survival of the Holocaust, bonded them for life. They committed themselves to starting a new life and a family after suffering such devastating loss. In 1952, my older sister, Chava (or Evie in English), was born, and I came along five years later.

Through the Jewish agency, my father learned that one of his five brothers had survived the war and had moved to New York. Shortly after hearing this news, my father sailed on a freight ship to the United States, where he and his brother were reunited. My uncle urged my father to join his business and bring the family over to the United States to ensure our safety and to provide us with a quality education and a better life. With much trepidation and sadness, my mother agreed and, in 1958, when I was a year old, my parents immigrated to the United States.

Initially, my mother's adjustment to life in the United States was very painful. She became depressed over leaving the country she had loved so dearly. Quickly realizing that life in the United States would be challenging, she began working in the travel industry for an established tour company. Eventually, she started her own agency in partnership with an old friend from Israel. Her business enabled her to travel at discounted rates to see family and friends in both Israel and England on a regular basis. She passed the discounted rates on to our family as well, which was a wonderful benefit to having her in the business. Both my sister and I inherited her passion for travel and exploited every opportunity to do so.

This narrative of how my parents grew up, separately made their way to Israel, joined the military, and later met and moved to the United States stuck with me until my mother's revelation about an ex-boyfriend. As I packed for my trip to Europe and Israel, which my parents had gifted me after my college graduation, she asked if I would be interested in meeting an "old flame" of hers while I visited family in London. I was dumbstruck. I was aware of my parents' histories, their survival stories, their experiences in Israel, and their decision to leave Israel and raise us as Americans. What I did not understand was where an English flame fit into the picture.

At my parents' kitchen table, my mother told me the story of Edward. When she was stationed in Egypt under British occupation, she met and fell in love with a British officer named Edward. As the occupiers, the British were reviled at the time, so my mother's peers did not support their romance, especially since Edward was not Jewish. Somewhere in that timeframe, my mother learned of her parents' and two younger sisters' deaths in the Holocaust. Overwhelmed with grief, she struggled with survivor's guilt. When the war was over, Edward prepared to return to England, where my mother's brother and cousins had settled. He asked my mother to marry him and start a new life with him there. She turned him down, and a heartbroken Edward returned to England without my mother, eventually got married, had two children, and became a journalist for a prominent newspaper in London. My mother tearfully explained to me that her guilt prevented her from marrying out of her faith. She felt that if she had married Edward, she would have betrayed her heritage and the memories of her family who had perished.

According to my mother, she and Edward reconnected during one of her frequent family visits to London. She was especially close to her cousin Hertel, who was a year younger and more like a sister than a cousin. Hertel had married Gerhard, another German refugee on the Kindertransport, and settled with him in North London. I planned to stay with them during my trip, as my mother always did. My mother offered me the chance to meet Edward, who was in his sixties, while I was there. Intrigued by her story and curious about the fellow my mother had fallen for before my father all those years ago, I agreed.

Hertel and Gerhard, whom I fondly referred to as my London "aunt" and "uncle," had a unique love relationship, one I always sought to emulate. They met as teenagers and essentially grew up together. Their two sons, David and Danny, were like brothers to me and my sister, and we grew up sharing all major life-cycle events with their family. I was thrilled to have an opportunity to stay with them again.

During my visit, Hertel drove me to Heathrow airport to meet Edward before my departure to Zurich. We were seated in the airport lounge having coffee when a dignified, gray-haired gentleman with blue eyes approached us, and we stood up to greet him. It was clear that Hertel and Edward had already met by their quiet acknowledgment of each other. When I looked Edward in the eye to thank him for coming, I could see how shaken up he was. Sweating profusely, he asked me to turn my head to the side so that he could view my profile. After I obliged, he exclaimed that I looked like a classic "Greek coin," just like my mother. That was the first time my prominent nose had been described in such glowing terms. I wasn't sure whether to be flattered or put off by his comment.

Once we sat down, Edward continued to harp on my resemblance to my mother, which made me increasingly uncomfortable. He also revealed to me that he still kept a lock of her copper-colored hair from more than twenty-five years earlier in a drawer. "She was an amazing, dynamic woman, a born leader," he explained. "Everyone looked up to her. We all loved and respected her." His remarks didn't seem to align with my mother's version of the public disapproval she experienced as a result of their relationship.

Once Edward wrapped up his journey down memory lane, we prepared to part ways. "I am honored to have met you," he said. "I would have liked to have spent some time taking you around the sights of London and up to Windsor Castle in the English countryside."

"What a shame that my time is so limited," I replied. "But I'm actually flying off to Switzerland in a few hours."

In truth, I wasn't sorry that I didn't have more time to spend with him. I found the entire experience to be very unsettling. It was clear how much Edward had loved, almost worshipped, my mother.

I felt profoundly sad for her. She had walked away from a man who appeared to be the "love of her life" out of an understandable sense of obligation to her own people. Her marriage to my father had been a sensible choice. He was a good and stable man, who had provided admirably for the family. While they were wonderful parents and completely loyal to each other, their marriage could hardly be described as a "love match." They would probably have been better off with different partners, partners who could have brought out the very best in each other. Instead, they were more like roommates.

They had come from two very different worlds. My mother was from an upper-middle-class family in Leipzig, Germany, which was known as a cultural center. My father was raised in a small village outside Warsaw, Poland, and didn't have the advantages my mother had had. While she spoke fluent English when they arrived in the United States, my father had to learn the language from scratch at forty years old. Their bond consisted primarily of keeping what little family they had left together and raising my sister and me to the best of their abilities. Their relationship clearly lacked the passion Edward had described between himself and my mother.

"Those kinds of relationships don't come along very often in life," I thought. "What a tragedy to have given up her chance at lifelong happiness. They appeared to have been each other's soul mates and should have stayed together."

I reasoned that if she had stayed with Edward, I would have never been born. Still, I loved and understood my mother enough to recognize what she had sacrificed for her values. I resolved not to let the same fate befall me.

## CHAPTER EIGHT

# The One Who Got Away

*A*lan was a tall and handsome bachelor who, at age fifty, sought my help to meet a woman whom he could marry. He was Jewish and had been raised in an intact family, where his parents doted on him and his older sister. After college, Alan forged a successful career in day trading, which he taught himself. His success afforded him the opportunity to purchase a large home in McLean, Virginia, at the age of thirty-five. While he had resided there for quite some time, he had yet to experience sharing his home with a woman, even though it could have easily accommodated a family of five.

Alan carried the shame of never being married with him, which deeply embarrassed him. As I listened to his story, I realized that the reason he felt so self-conscious about this fact was because he had had an opportunity to pursue his version of the "perfect woman" while he was younger but declined to take the risk at the time and thus felt like a failure on some fundamental level.

While in his late twenties, Alan traveled to Paris one summer to visit a couple whom he had been friends with since college. The

55

couple had relocated to France just five years earlier. Eager to see
their old friend, they invited Alan to stay with them, explore the
city, and meet some friends within their social circle. Alan readily
accepted the invitation and set about planning the various sights
he would visit, both locally and along the French countryside. He
had studied French in high school and college and looked forward
to the opportunity to practice the language he adored but was no
longer fluent in.

Alan's friends were thrilled to have him and arranged tickets
to various museums and special events in town for their visit.
On Bastille Day, they set out to watch fireworks with a group
of expatriates whom they had gotten friendly with. The couple
introduced Alan to a woman in the group named Lily, the sister
of a friend from New York who had studied at the Sorbonne, a
renowned university in Paris's Latin Quarter. Lily had fallen in
love with Paris and decided to remain there and pursue a career
in journalism.

Alan was immediately taken with Lily. She was outgoing,
vivacious, and sweet. Physically, she was just his type, a tall,
graceful brunette with long, dark, curly hair. Alan couldn't believe
his good fortune when Lily's sister told him that Lily was single,
having broken up with a fellow, whom she had dated for years,
about six months earlier. Lily was attracted to Alan as well, and
they ended up spending the entire evening huddled together, to the
exclusion of the rest of their crowd. Although their friends hadn't
actually planned to fix them up, they heartily approved of this new
development and encouraged Alan to spend as much time with
Lily as possible while he was in Paris.

Not needing much encouragement, they spent nearly every
day together during Alan's stay. Lily was off from school for the
summer and could therefore take the time to show Alan around
and give him the exposure to the city that only a native could
provide. Alan was smitten with both Lily and Paris, never wanting

to return home. She was the girl of his dreams; she was stylish and exuded a quiet confidence and sex appeal that Alan found irresistible.

As the time for Alan to return home drew nearer, they began to discuss how they might keep their new romance alive. Lily was bold enough to suggest that she spend an extended period of time with Alan in the DC area. She was in a position to take a sabbatical from teaching and willing to give their relationship a "trial run" in order to figure out whether marriage might be in the cards for them.

Touched and overwhelmed by Lily's emotional honesty and desire to be with him, Alan felt terrified about making a mistake. If it didn't work out, Lily would be dependent on him. When he thought about the glamorous life she led in Paris, he worried that he might disappoint her.

While Alan made great money, he didn't think he could measure up to Lily's expectations or provide her with the kind of life she'd find stimulating enough. He reasoned that if it didn't work out, he would be plagued with guilt about encouraging her to leave the country she had grown to love. He saw their relationship as an exciting summer love, but not one that could sustain itself through the everyday stresses and strains of marriage and children. As a result, he turned her down, suggesting she plan a brief visit in the fall instead. Lily felt crushed that his feelings for her didn't match up to hers and that he didn't try to figure out a more permanent arrangement. Heartbroken, she ended things between them a few days before his departure.

Since then, Alan thought of Lily as "the one who got away," not recognizing that *he* had made the decision himself and alone bore the responsibility of not pursuing a love he hadn't experienced before or since. His fears had prevented him from taking the plunge, for better or worse, to explore whether he and Lily could make a go of it.

I introduced Alan to several very desirable women, most of whom were in their forties, during our year-long contract; however, it became apparent to me that even though he and Lily had dated over twenty years earlier, no one could hold a candle to Lily in his mind. I was therefore unsuccessful in finding Alan a wife, despite my best efforts to convince him that his comparisons of a young Lily to these women were self-defeating and unfair. As a result, I found myself thinking that Alan, not unlike my mother, had not allowed himself to take a chance on love out of fear, insecurity, and in my mother's case, survivor's guilt. The worst outcome for Alan would have been divorce, but never knowing what could have been between him and Lily seemed like an even worse burden for him to carry around forever.

## CHAPTER NINE

# Caught Me a Catch

*I* n the spring of 1981, I enrolled in summer school after
my second year at Hofstra Law so that I could graduate
a semester early. After graduation, I planned to go to London to
work for an organization called Prisoner's Abroad, which I had
learned of through my connections in the Philadelphia criminal
defense community. Prisoner's Abroad provided access to legal
and social services to clients, mostly British nationals, who were
imprisoned in foreign countries. Most clients were charged with
drug smuggling, and many had trumped-up charges in third-world
countries. I hoped to join their team to assist Americans in need
of similar resources. Given that it was a volunteer position, I also
hoped to find paid employment with a criminal defense attorney in
London to cover my expenses while there.

My last semester at Hofstra was ridiculously busy. I had to
complete all of my academic requirements, study for the New York
bar, and plan my London trip postgraduation. For the most part, I
didn't date so I could focus on my studies.

Romance wasn't completely off my radar that semester, however. My family friend Ari and I had dabbled in a short-lived relationship while he was visiting from Israel. We packed some very fun and crazy times into our three months together, but our timing was completely off. He was still dating other people, which made things between us complicated and messy. Knowing myself enough to know that I would probably get hurt, I decided to end things between us. Also, I had managed to hide the physical part of our relationship from my parents and wanted to keep it that way. My hope was that we could maintain a friendship, given the family connection between us.

In October of that year, out of the blue, I got a call from my old college friend named Howard, who was now living in Washington, DC, working for a tax law firm. He'd been a friend of Gary's, my first boyfriend at Penn, so I had known him quite well. I was surprised to hear from him. He called to say that he was planning to attend a Halloween party in Philly, thrown by some friends of his from Penn, and invited me to attend. I wasn't sure how to take the invitation. I wondered whether it was a date or just a friendly social invitation. Either way, I decided it would be a fun break from the grind. I was also happy to have a reason to get back to Philly. I hadn't been there since my last visit with Claud, which wasn't a particularly happy memory.

I borrowed a Southern belle Halloween costume from Sharon, my former boss and friend in Philly, who had an extensive collection of varied and dramatic wardrobe items. I completed the costume with a long brown straight wig that covered my curly auburn hair. This was especially fun since my hair had always been rather wild, and I had often fantasized about having long, silky straight hair. I also donned a floppy hat over the wig and wore a long, flowy, off-the-shoulder flowered gown that accentuated my curves. After not seeing me for years, Howard barely recognized me in my getup at first, but I could tell he heartily approved. He came dressed as a cowboy in a plaid shirt, jeans, and boots with spurs.

Howard had changed since Penn. He had cut off his "Jewfro" and now sported a short haircut and wire-framed glasses. His quite handsome face was now more visible. At Penn, he'd hidden himself beneath his hair and thick-framed glasses due to his shyness. Now that he worked as a young attorney, he had to conform to a more conservative look, which was actually more flattering to him.

As old friends, there was an instant feeling of comfort between us. We had a great time partying and dancing through the wee hours of the morning. When the party ended, I called a taxi to take me back to Sharon's house, where I was staying.

"Let's stay in touch," Howard said as he hugged me goodbye.

I didn't know exactly what to make of it, but Howard had lingered a little too long in the hug for me to think that his interest was purely platonic.

The next day, I called Peter, who was Howard's friend from Penn.

"You'll never guess who I heard from," I exclaimed.

"Who?" Peter asked.

"Howard! He called out of the blue and invited me to a party in Philly, so I decided to go. It was so much fun. By the way, Howard looks completely different these days. He's much cuter than I remember and he has really matured. He was actually a lot of fun to hang out with," I reported.

"Did you guys make plans to get together again?" he asked.

"No," I said. "We kind of left it up in the air."

"Why don't you invite him up for a weekend?" Peter asked.

"Whoa, that's a pretty dramatic step up from just one date, if you could even call it that," I responded.

"Do you like him?" Peter persisted.

"Yes, I suppose so," I replied. "I just never saw him as a potential boyfriend."

"Well, Howard has always been really shy, as you know. He just needs some encouragement," Peter explained. "Invite him up for a weekend. If he says yes, you'll just take it from there."

"Really?" I asked. "You don't think that's being way too forward?"

"Hell no!" he responded. "I think he'll be totally flattered and thrilled. The worst he can say is no. I doubt he will, though. I always thought he had a bit of a crush on you. Of course, he never would have acted on it while you were with Gary. But now, there's nothing standing in the way."

I pondered this further. I wasn't sure whether or not Peter was pushing this out of guilt for having "spilled the beans" on Claud's involvement with another woman. He was such a good friend and knew how much his unintended disclosure had hurt me. Perhaps he was trying to make amends to me now.

"I'll think it over," I told him.

"Don't think too long," he said. "The holidays are coming up. How about inviting him for New Year's weekend? I'm sure he doesn't have a date."

"Hmmm. That would be quite a way to ring in the new year," I joked. He agreed.

I took my courage in hand and extended the invitation to Howard the next time he called me. He'd called me regularly since the party, and I enjoyed the attention.

"Do you have plans for New Year's?" I asked.

"No," he answered tentatively.

"How about coming up for the weekend then?" I ventured. There was a long pause.

"That would be great!" he finally responded.

"Wonderful," I said. "That gives me something to look forward to, with everything else going on. Can't wait!" I exclaimed and quickly ended the call. While I was delighted that Howard had said yes, I had no idea what to expect and figured that, at the very worst, it would just be a weekend between old friends. I reassured myself that since he wasn't a close friend, it wouldn't be that big of a deal if things didn't work out.

The time between then and New Year's weekend sped by. I had gone into the city to stay at my parents' house for Christmas weekend and then returned to my home in Hempstead, New York, to await Howard's arrival. He took the train up from DC then switched for the Long Island Railroad to Hempstead where I met him at the station. We were happy to see each other and greeted each other warmly with hugs and kisses on the cheek. I took him back to the house and introduced him to my roommates. We then settled into my room for the weekend. It was awkward at first, and I knew I'd have to be very careful, given how shy he was.

"Okay if I kiss you?" I asked.

He didn't answer. Instead, he simply approached and kissed me tenderly on the lips. It was a very sweet beginning.

I knew that Howard didn't have much experience with women while at Penn, and he hadn't mentioned any relationships since then. I told myself that I'd have to be the one to lead. We went out for a festive New Year's dinner and returned to my room, feeling rather tipsy after several glasses of champagne. We naturally fell into my bed, where he was as eager as a puppy, trying to please me in every way. Thankfully, we passed the chemistry test with flying colors.

It was both a lazy and passionate holiday weekend. It felt lighthearted and fun to be together. In the middle of our second night together, while we were fast asleep, the house cat named Bill began meowing loudly. It was common for Bill to roam the neighborhood nightly and return with all kinds of battle wounds. Despite this, it never stopped him from venturing out. Since my bedroom was closest to the door, I usually got up to let him outside. As I groaned and made a move to get up, Howard stopped me and said, "I'll do it. Don't worry. You can stay put."

Sure enough, he got out of my warm bed to brave the unheated hallway and open the front door for Bill. I lay there thinking, "Now here's a guy who would get up with the babies. He just might be 'a keeper.'"

By the end of the weekend, I was optimistic and Howard was smitten. Despite our newly blossoming relationship, I was determined to follow through on my plans to spend six months in London after I graduated and took the bar at the end of February. I wasn't going to let a new boyfriend derail my plans. While Howard was disappointed that I'd be so far away for so long, he was completely supportive of my plans and gave me regular pep talks as I studied for the bar. He'd been through the same ordeal, having taken the DC bar, and therefore was a very helpful coach.

When the time came for me to leave for London, Howard and I resolved to keep in touch. In line with the days before the Internet and cell phones, we planned to speak weekly from my landline in London. The phone appointment needed to accommodate the time difference, of course. In between, we chose to record letters to each other on mini cassette tapes so that we could hear each other's voices and thus stay connected.

Howard and I grew closer and closer during this time as I shared my experiences in London with him. He, in turn, began to overcome his shyness and open himself up to me emotionally. This touched me deeply. I began to miss him terribly, so, after a few months, he offered to fly over and visit me. Thrilled by his grand gesture, I decided not only to show him London but also Paris. I arranged a long, romantic weekend for two, where we planned to tour the city and see the main attractions, including the Eiffel Tower, Notre Dame, and the world-famous museums. This would be an adventure for us both.

The next few months went by in a whirlwind, during which time I juggled two part-time jobs and spent plenty of time with my uncle, aunt, and four cousins, all of whom I had grown even closer to during my stay. I told them all about Howard and looked forward to introducing him to them as his visit drew near.

Although I told her how brilliant of an attorney he was, Aunt Hertel had her doubts about Howard. He got off on the wrong foot initially because he couldn't seem to get the time difference straight. Not realizing that London was five hours ahead of Washington, he called several times in the middle of the night, waking both Aunt Hertel and her husband. When he finally did make an appearance in London, she was surprised that he was so soft spoken.

I was thrilled to see him again. We spent a few days in London then flew to Paris where neither of us had been before. Sadly, I was afflicted with a terrible migraine attack while there, and Howard showed remarkable empathy and caring during that episode, which I took as a wonderful sign.

One evening, Howard annoyed a restaurant proprietor by insisting that we sit at a table overlooking the Eiffel Tower. Once seated and enjoying the ambiance, Howard haltingly asked me if I would consider moving to Washington and living with him upon my return from London. I was touched but conflicted. In my heart of hearts, I really wanted to be married and wondered whether it was a good idea to live together first or not. I knew of several couples who had lived together and whose relationships had fallen apart a few years later. Would being married make a difference? I felt too vulnerable to share my concerns with him and simply said that I was flattered but needed to think about it. Deep inside, I was disappointed that,

*I was disappointed that, in the most romantic city in the world, I received a nonproposal of sorts.*

in the most romantic city in the world, I received a nonproposal of sorts.

We returned to London after three days and took a road trip to Wales to do some hiking in the countryside. We were in the Forest of Dean preparing a picnic lunch when I desperately needed to pee. We were quite far from any public bathrooms, so I pulled some tissues out of my knapsack, spotted the right tree, and, to his surprise and amusement, dropped my drawers right there and did my thing. Afterward, when we got settled on our picnic blanket, Howard pulled a pouch out of his jean's pocket and, to my astonishment, removed a diamond engagement ring. He proposed to me then and there. Shocked and overwhelmed with emotion, I readily agreed. After hugging and kissing each other passionately, I asked him why he had suggested living together when we were in Paris rather than proposing. He explained that he wasn't entirely sure himself and wanted to "go in stages." He had traveled across the Atlantic with a ring but hadn't felt secure enough in the relationship to venture there in Paris. Yet, in Wales, after watching me spontaneously relieve myself, he was convinced. I thought that was a bit strange but didn't care. I had finally gotten the romantic proposal I had dreamed of. We would soon start a brand-new life together in an exciting city. I couldn't have been happier.

## CHAPTER TEN

# One Person's Trash Is Another's Treasure

Zack and Shelly were childhood sweethearts. They both grew up in the greater New York area and attended sleep-away camp together in the Catskills from the ages of thirteen to seventeen, and both became camp counselors as well. Although they went to different high schools, they saw each other frequently during the school year and remained a couple throughout their college years, each attending local city colleges.

After graduating college, they got married and began a family within two years, ultimately having two sons and a daughter within a five-year period. Their family and friends rejoiced in their good fortune. Zack went on to medical school while Shelly worked full time in the accounting field to support the family. They had a good life together and were blessed that their children were all healthy and well adjusted.

Zack reached out to me for my matchmaking services only three months after he and Shelly had separated after a twenty-five-year marriage. He explained his circumstances and inquired as to whether I'd consider working with him. I explained that I had a policy of not accepting clients into my active membership who aren't legally divorced, for obvious reasons. We continued to chat further, and I was impressed with his honesty, self-awareness, and desire to move on to a healthy relationship. I let him know that when the time was right, I would happily work with him. In the meantime, if he wanted to join my database, there might be someone in my network who would consider dating a separated man, if they themselves were not seeking marriage in the immediate future. That made sense to Zack, and we agreed to meet for coffee the following week.

Zack was tall and had an imposing presence when he walked into the Starbucks in Bethesda for our initial meeting. We found a private spot and proceeded to become acquainted. He had an endearing, somewhat humble quality about him, despite his success as an orthopedic surgeon.

Zack explained that he and Shelly had had a very successful marriage for many years, but somehow the emotional intimacy had gotten bleached out of their marriage over the decades as he focused on his career and she occupied the role of primary parent. While they did all the customary things together as a family, celebrating holidays and taking interesting and fun vacations, their life as a couple had begun to stagnate.

Shelly enjoyed entertaining friends and taking advantage of the arts in town, while Zack enjoyed sports. He coached Little League on the weekends and enjoyed attending games and going skiing with his buddies whenever he was able to get away. The physical chemistry between them had always been "fine," as he put it, but both of them seemed to have lost interest in each other sexually over the years. They had become more like roommates than lovers, and they were both frustrated and depressed over that development.

Eventually, Shelly asked for a trial separation. Zack told me that if she hadn't asked first, he would have done so in the near future. He told me that he really hadn't been happy in the marriage for the past ten years and that he felt strongly that there must be someone better suited for him out there. He assured me that there was no chance of him and Shelly reconciling but that they remained good friends and committed to being present for their children, two of whom were still living with Shelly in the family home. Zack had rented an apartment nearby and was adjusting to his new single life. He stated that he and Shelly had decided not to file for divorce anytime soon for financial reasons, but if he met and got serious with anyone within the next year or so, he would be prepared to file sooner. This would assure anyone he got involved with that he would be fully prepared to become legally available to consider remarriage.

Zack was happy to join my database as an interim measure. I reached out to two women, the first of whom declined to meet Zack given his circumstances. I completely understood and informed Zack of that effort on my part. Erica, the second woman I contacted, had just ended a four-year relationship three months earlier. She was still recovering from that loss, so she was in no hurry to get serious with anyone new but found Zack's photo to be very appealing and agreed to meet him.

Erica and Zack had a fabulous first date. He texted me the next morning to thank me for the referral and said, "Leora, you hit the nail on the head with Erica." She found him to be bright, charming, and fun and laughed at the unexpected outcome of liking him so quickly.

They began seeing each other at least twice a week. Erica phoned me for advice once Zack began to pressure her to spend more time with him. He offered to meet her ten-year-old son during a vacation week when he would be with her for the duration. I coached Erica to set her own pace for spending time

with Zack and encouraged her to wait several more months
to introduce her son to him until she knew the direction her
relationship with Zack was heading in. This felt far too rushed to
be healthy. Erica appreciated my feedback and resolved to take
more control over the situation with Zack.

A month later, Erica called to say that she had ended things
with Zack. She told me that he had shared with her a recent
conversation that he'd had with Shelly, wherein he told Shelly
that he was dating someone. Shelly seemed to have trouble
with that and called a few days later to ask him whether he'd
consider trying again. Apparently, once Shelly became aware
that another woman was interested in Zack, he didn't seem too
bad, and she began to second-guess herself over her decision to
end their marriage.

Erica wisely decided that this scenario would not be healthy
for her and wished Zack well in his resolution with Shelly. She
wasn't angry or bitter, just empathetic with Zack's plight and clear
with him that he needed time to figure things out without the
complication of dating her. She told him that the timing was just
not in their favor, but if he eventually did go ahead and file for
divorce and she was still single, she was open to revisiting things
with him. He was disappointed but understood completely.

Whether Zack and Shelly will successfully reconcile is still
an unknown. In my professional
experience, when couples meet and
marry so young in life, they often grow
apart as they navigate life's challenges.
It takes a major effort to maintain the
emotional and physical intimacy in a
marriage; couples who haven't worked
at maintaining that bond over the years
often find that when the kids are eventually grown and out of the
house, they have become lost to each other.

> **When couples meet and marry so young in life, they often grow apart as they navigate life's challenges.**

Early in my marriage to Howard, while I had the optimism of youth, I believed that we would conquer everything. I also knew, however, that it was impossible to predict which direction things would head in or whether we'd stand the test of time.

## CHAPTER ELEVEN

# British Invasion

*I* arrived in London, suitcases in hand, in March 1982. I planned to stay with Hertel and Gerhard until I found a place of my own. While I loved my English family, I didn't want to be a burden to them during my six months living in London. I was happy to visit them often but preferred to be independent to prevent any undue pressure on the wonderful relationship we enjoyed. Hertel agreed and began scouring the papers for the right living situation for me. She identified a room available in a house nearby with three roommates who were seeking a fourth. She drove me over to meet them, and we hit it off immediately. The women were all close to my age and Jewish, so we had that in common. One roommate was a tall blonde from London who worked for a marketing company. Another was an adorable, petite brunette from Wales who worked for an accounting firm. The newest roommate was a schoolteacher from Leeds. The chemistry between us was immediate, and I moved in with them shortly thereafter.

Once settled, I paid a visit to Prisoner's Abroad. I was so confident that they would welcome my offer to volunteer that I hadn't even written in advance to inquire about the possibility of doing so. I was dismayed when I got to their office. They operated out of a single room in a walk-up that housed several other organizations in a rather seedy part of London. Even if they agreed to let me work with them, the space was too small for me to set up another workstation. Regardless, I walked in with my resume in hand, full of enthusiasm, and expressed my interest in working with them. I offered several ideas about how I could add value to their organization.

The codirectors, Greg and Jill, had run the organization for quite some time and weren't really looking for help, but they agreed to discuss the idea further. They didn't seem all that enthused with my offer but did take the time to explain their work. They stated that the current office space was temporary and that they would be moving to a larger space very shortly, so there would be room for me to have a permanent desk if I decided to join them. In the meantime, I would need to alternate sharing space with each of them, as one or both were usually out on appointments during the day. With that, Greg handed my resume back to me and suggested that over the upcoming holiday weekend I digest what they had shared and, only afterward, let them know if I still wanted to move forward. In the meantime, they would confer with each other before making a final decision.

I liked them both. Jill, who was in her late forties, had a former boyfriend who had committed suicide after serving time in a Turkish prison for attempting to smuggle hashish as a younger man. He had been so traumatized by his years of incarceration that he jumped in front of a British Rail train one day. As a result, she was extremely passionate about the work. Greg was about thirty, small in stature, with curly brown hair. He seemed full of spirit and energy and didn't really know what to make of the American woman sitting in front of him.

I was a bit crestfallen that they hadn't jumped at the chance to have me onboard, but I took their advice and spent the weekend thinking it over. I wondered if I hadn't made a terrible mistake. I had been so caught up with the idea of working with them and having this job on my resume that I hadn't even considered how the logistics of my plan would work. It felt much less glamorous than what I had envisioned. Nevertheless, I decided to give it a try since I had a good feeling about Jill and Greg and was determined not to look like a quitter. I informed them that I was also seeking paid employment with a criminal attorney and would be juggling both positions if I succeeded. They were comfortable with this arrangement.

I had come armed with a list of London criminal practitioners and began checking them off as I pounded the pavement for paid employment. My uncle Lothar was a very successful businessman in London and offered to find me work with his corporate attorneys. He warned that it would be virtually impossible for me to find work on my own since such work was scarce, especially since I did not have the proper documentation to work there legally. I declined his offer, maintaining my desire to focus on criminal law. Sure enough, my efforts to find a job were painstaking and frustrating. Several of the attorneys whom I approached asked me out, but none of them had any open positions.

One day, as I sat on the London Underground en route to the next law office, I noticed a fellow sitting to my right reading the *Law Society Journal*. I peered over his shoulder to read what I could. As I did, he turned to me, looking quite annoyed that I had invaded his personal space. I read his body language and immediately apologized for the intrusion. I explained that I had just graduated law school in the States and was interested in current events within the local legal community. After accepting my apology, he informed me that he and his partner had successfully employed several Americans at their firm in the past and were actually looking to hire a clerk to help them prepare for some upcoming trials. He invited me to meet with him and his partner that very week. Delighted by his offer, I readily agreed to follow up with them at once.

When I arrived at the law firm on Harewood Place in London, I was immediately impressed. The building was an architectural marvel, a gracious London postwar building behind London's busy Oxford Street that stood out among the more modern buildings nearby. A receptionist ushered me into the office of the senior partner, a short, bearded, charismatic man in his forties. My "Underground companion," Clive, the partner whom I had met on the subway, was also present. After a brief introduction, they proceeded to tell me about the upcoming trials that they were preparing for and how I could potentially fit in.

Due to England's bifurcated legal system, once a solicitor prepared a case for court, a barrister would then argue the case at trial. English law required the solicitor to have a representative in court to observe the proceedings, even though the solicitor would no longer actively handle the case. It didn't make financial sense for the actual solicitor to sit in court for that purpose, so they hired clerks to fulfill this requirement. The clerk's responsibility was to function as a liaison between the barrister, the client, and the solicitor's firm. The clerk would summarize court proceedings and then report back to the solicitor.

Since time was of the essence, they hired me on the spot. I was thrilled to have such an incredible opportunity to witness the barristers at work. It was legal theater for me, and to get paid for doing so was a dream come true.

I spent the next few months juggling my volunteer work for Prisoners Abroad with the law firm's cases in court. It was a hectic but rewarding time. Jill, Greg, and I would hit the pub at the end of each workday. There, we gradually got to know one another and soon became close friends. Their initial impressions of me as a hyper American began to fade as they developed a deeper appreciation for who I really was.

One day, a tall, handsome fellow with piercing blue eyes walked in the door. Ian, who was a board member of Prisoners Abroad, seemed quite delighted to meet me. He was a bright, warm, charismatic fellow with a South London accent, and I took to him immediately. Jill and Greg then suggested that Ian and I attend an event that evening where we would represent the organization since neither of them could attend. I agreed to accompany Ian.

We did an admirable job of representing our organization at the meeting, which ended in the early evening. Afterward, Ian suggested that we see a new comedy that had opened in a nearby movie theater, so we headed over there together. I wondered whether Jill and Greg had attempted to "play matchmaker" by sending us on this mission together. "They know I have a boyfriend in Washington, DC, so why would they go there?" I asked myself. I concluded that they had no agenda after all and decided to relax and enjoy the evening with Ian, who was completely charming the entire time. While I was pleasant enough, I chose not to put out any romantic signals. I did not want him to get the wrong impression.

Toward the end of my stay in London, Ian asked if he could take me out for a farewell dinner. By then, we had spent enough time around each other to have become casual friends, and I was happy to have a chance to spend some quality time with him before I returned home. Ian was not aware of my engagement to Howard that summer, and he was surprised when I showed him my ring and shared my plans to move to Washington, DC, upon my return to the States.

After congratulating me, Ian proclaimed, "I really didn't see you as the marrying type, Leora!" I wasn't quite sure how to take that comment.

"Well, whether I'm the type or not, that's my plan," I replied.

We spoke further about my courtship with Howard in all its complexities, and I was able to articulate all of my feelings, hopes, and even doubts to Ian that evening. As we continued to talk, I felt surprised to feel romantic chemistry creeping in between us. Ian must've felt the chemistry, too, because over dinner he blurted out, "We should have had an affair while you were here. Why didn't we?"

I answered Ian as best as I could. "I wasn't looking to get involved with anyone else while I was here. I've been seeing Howard, and my loyalty to him prevented me from being open to it." I then acknowledged the growing chemistry between us and my belief that anything else between us was apparently not "meant to be."

Ian presented me with a lovely silver bracelet as a going-away gift. After dinner, he suggested that we take a walk in nearby Regents Park. We walked arm in arm for some time, talking nonstop the entire evening. We had an amazing conversation, one I hadn't even come close to having with Howard, the man I was planning to marry. I soon found myself regretting that we hadn't had the affair he spoke of. By the end of the evening, I felt an unexpected, profound sadness at having to say goodbye.

In the fall of 1982, I returned from London and, after making the rounds among my New York family and friends, packed up and moved to Washington, DC. While I was still in London, Howard had rented us an apartment in the trendy Dupont Circle area, which was populated with many young couples like us. Located on the top floor of a renovated multi-apartment townhouse, our apartment was charming but tiny. It had a deck three times its size. While nice to look at, the deck didn't get much use, however, due to the DC weather conditions, which I gradually adjusted to. We had no closet space either.

I felt increasingly claustrophobic in the apartment. I studied for the DC bar during the day while Howard worked downtown for a tax law firm. The firm had hired him straight out of Georgetown Law, where Howard held the prestigious position of editor of the *Law Review*.

That winter, we were mugged at gunpoint in the alley behind our townhouse, where we parked our car. The perpetrator robbed us of whatever cash we had on us and removed my diamond ring from my trembling finger. "Was this a sign?" I asked myself, traumatized over the event that had just unfolded. I dismissed this thought as a symptom of the shock I was in. I was deeply upset to have lost my ring, which Howard had insured and promised to replace. True to his word, he replaced the ring with a similarly sized diamond, despite the fact that the stone was smaller than I would have liked. In fact, his grandmother Molly chastised him, saying he should "be ashamed of himself" for buying me such a small diamond. I didn't want to appear materialistic and was grateful to him for keeping his word. Shortly after this incident, Howard and I moved to Woodley Park into a large, airy apartment overlooking the National Zoo with less charm but with much more closet space.

On May 1, 1983, we were married in Brooklyn, New York, in front of nearly two hundred people. My London family as well as relatives as far away as Israel and Brazil came over for the event. My parents were beaming with pride for "marrying off" their youngest daughter. Howard and I honeymooned in Israel, courtesy of my mother, the travel agent. A year later, we began to try to start a family, and I was fortunate to become pregnant soon thereafter. We decided to buy a house with our wedding money, which each of our parents supplemented as well. It was a struggle agreeing on a house that suited us both. In fact, our real estate agent nearly switched careers after working with us, but we finally found one within our budget in the Maryland suburbs that worked for us both. We moved in one month before our daughter, Elana, was born. Three years later, Adam came along. It seemed as if we were the perfect family. We now had our dream home, two beautiful children, promising careers, and presumably bright futures.

## CHAPTER TWELVE

# An Unhealthy Affair

Ten years after I left London and was running what was by then an established matchmaking company, an Englishwoman in her early thirties consulted me for my services. She had never been married, had no children, and hoped to meet a divorced man with children so she could experience stepchildren in her life. Her story was a compelling one, especially given my history in England.

Nora was a beautiful and brilliant economist who grew up in North London and had a wide circle of family and friends. She was successful, popular, and had a magnetic personality. One holiday season, she was invited to a friend's party where she met a very handsome barrister named Ben, who was about fifteen years her senior.

As their conversation deepened, Ben and Nora became quite flirtatious, until an attractive older woman named Mary approached and introduced herself to Nora as Ben's wife. Nora did her best to hide her surprise and disappointment that Ben was married and continued the conversation with the two of them as a couple. As quickly as was socially appropriate, she moved on to speak to the other people in the room.

As the evening progressed, she noticed Ben's continued stares in her direction and realized that he was heading back toward her to re-engage her in conversation, along with some other friends Nora had been chatting with. Mary moved on to another conversation, leaving Ben and Nora free to talk further. Nora introduced Ben to some of her friends, and they continued their cocktail party chatter with the group.

It was clear to Nora that Ben was continuing to flirt with her, despite being married and having his wife in the same room, which concerned and troubled Nora. While she found him to be very seductive, she certainly did not want to get involved with a married man, especially one who showed so little respect toward his wife. She felt unsettled and made an early exit in order to avoid Ben for the rest of the evening.

The next business day, Nora was surprised by a phone call from Ben at her office. She immediately recalled exchanging cards when she and Ben were first alone, shortly before she met Ben's wife. Before she could muster the courage to tell him to lose her number, he quickly invited her to lunch "for business purposes," and, to her own astonishment, she agreed to meet him in the West End near both their offices.

Their lunch eventually morphed into an affair that lasted almost fifteen years. They fell deeply in love. Ben kept promising Nora that he would leave Mary for her, knowing how much Nora craved marriage and children, but he never did fulfill that promise. After Nora had devoted her childbearing years to her relationship with Ben, she finally came to the realization that nothing would ever change and decided to leave Ben and immigrate to the United States to start a new life. Because she was so accomplished professionally, she was able to secure an impressive position at the World Bank, an international financial institution that provides loans to foreign countries for capital projects.

As a very desirable client, it was easy for me to fix up Nora with several interesting and eligible men. A few months into the process, however, it became clear that Nora was still mourning her relationship with Ben and was therefore unable to give anyone else fair consideration. As her relationship coach, I encouraged her to take a break from meeting people and to put her membership on hold while she worked with a skilled therapist whom I recommended to address the lingering effects of her relationship with Ben. She reluctantly agreed and spent the next six months seeing a therapist weekly to come to terms with the fifteen-year affair that had prevented her from marrying during a time in her life when she could have easily found a husband and had a family of her own. I wondered which one of us was better off, me for not allowing myself to give into my feelings for Ian while I was in London and still a "free agent" or Nora, who had thrown caution to the wind with Ben only to have been cheated out of the best childbearing years of her life.

Eventually, Nora reactivated her membership, and I introduced her to Jeffrey, a handsome accountant in his own practice with three children, one a teenager and two who were already in college. By then, Nora's heart had opened to someone new, and she fell for Jeffrey's kindness, generosity, and willingness to include her into his family in an organic way. They were together for over five years, allowing Nora to experience a dynamic she had always craved. She and Jeffrey eventually parted amicably, and Nora continues to interact with Jeffrey's children, having bonded with them during a developmentally significant time in their lives.

## CHAPTER THIRTEEN

# From Lawyer to Love Broker

"What? You want to start a matchmaking business!" my mother exclaimed loudly into the phone after I shared my new business idea with her. "All that education we gave you," her German-accented voice becoming more strident, "you're going to just throw it away?"

"Mom," I said, "I'm not throwing anything away." She was referring to my Ivy League college education and a hard-earned law degree. "My education and job experience as a lawyer is part of me now and will only make me better at what I do."

My mother wasn't convinced. I knew the only way to get her onboard with the idea would be for me to plunge in and have her see me succeed.

I had practiced law for five years, in between having Elana and Adam. After Adam's birth and during my maternity leave, I sat nursing Adam as I pondered what my next steps would be professionally. I had been working for a federal regulatory agency,

CFTC, three days a week as an attorney in the trading and markets division, reviewing disclosure documents all day long. I knew it was not my calling, but part-time legal jobs in DC were scarce, so I grabbed this one, knowing that it would give me time with my young children. After working there since Elana had turned two and up through Adam's birth, I was eager for a change. It seemed as if the options in law were either to do something interesting and fulfilling like litigation, which was much more than a full-time job, or to sacrifice job fulfillment for regular hours. Neither spoke to me through my hormonal haze. Then, with one simple phone call, my career focus began to change.

One evening, Evie, my older sister who lived in Manhattan, called. She was divorced and seeking a quality man. "I'm thinking of doing something different," she began. "I'm thinking of hiring a matchmaker." She went on to describe a particular service on Madison Avenue, which was very exclusive and pricey. "Their fees begin at twenty thousand dollars per contract and go up from there," she explained, "but you get introduced to highly successful men."

My first instinct was one of caution. "I'd be wary of any service that charges that kind of money," I told her, "but you just gave me a brainstorm for my next career!" I exclaimed.

"What kind of crisis are you having with your profession?" my psychologist sister asked.

"Never mind that," I said. "I don't know of anyone in my area doing this kind of work. With the number of single professionals here, I think a business like that could really work!" My instincts told me that I was on to something.

From the time I began to socialize, even as a young child, I seemed to inspire people's confidence. Oddly, strangers on public transportation in Brooklyn would approach me and tell me their troubles. I listened sympathetically and tried to make them feel better for having shared their innermost feelings with me. I knew this quality would work for me as a matchmaker. Plus, I was a total romantic. I loved the idea of love. As early as age three, I had a boyfriend whom I knew from the stoop of my building on Argyle Road in Brooklyn, where we had lived upon arriving from Israel two years prior. He was an "older man" at age five who lived in the next building. His name was Lewis, and he was Jewish, so he chose me over Mary Beth, my Protestant friend and neighbor. My glory didn't last long, however. Lewis and his family were upwardly mobile and moved to Long

*Romantic drama was therefore bred into my bones at an early age.*

Island not even a year later, which resulted in my first heartbreak. Romantic drama was therefore bred into my bones at an early age.

Next came Yaron, an Israeli boy who was a year ahead of me at my Jewish day school. He approached me on the playground at recess and asked me to be his girlfriend. I was thrilled. He'd send me elaborate love letters filled with drawings depicting his feelings for me, which my sister discovered and teased me about. I didn't care. I was "in love." Yaron would ride his bike over to my apartment, and we would hang out on the stoop or walk to nearby Prospect Park. I reveled in my status as his girlfriend and gained a sense of confidence with boys. This, of course, served me well throughout my formative years. Interestingly, years later, at ages eleven and thirteen, respectively, Yaron and I attended the same sleepaway camp, Camp Kindervelt. I was his date for the Color War Victory Dance (or VD Dance, as it was known). He shocked me at the end of the evening by French kissing me on the front porch of my bunk, something I had never experienced before. I was both confused and excited, with a vague sense of what was yet to come.

## CHAPTER FOURTEEN

# Thinking Outside the Box

*I*n September 1989, with my husband Howard's blessing, advice from a business consultant, and the encouragement of colleagues and friends, I set about establishing my matchmaking business. I understood that word of mouth would be the key to my success, so I circulated in as many singles' networks as I could. One of the events I attended was the annual Singles' Expo at the Jewish Community Center in Rockville, Maryland, where I offered free boxes of truffles to participants who completed my market survey form. I hoped to accumulate a pool of singles who would be open to meeting my clients once I launched my business. One of the respondents was David, a cute and funny accountant in his early forties who had never been married. I liked his personality and followed up with him from the survey form. I invited him to meet me for dinner so that I could further screen him as a prospect for future clients.

David and I met in a casual restaurant in a DC neighborhood called Adams Morgan. As I settled into my chair, David said, "Leora, I have to be honest with you. I don't know if I'd be appropriate for your network."

"Oh?" I replied, encouraging him to continue.

"Well, before we start," he blurted, "I should tell you that I've done time."

"Oh my God!" I thought, "What's he going to tell me next? Is he a violent criminal or a sex offender?" I tried not to look rattled by this disclosure and invited him to explain.

He spent the next hour telling me that he'd been an A student throughout his academic career and got a fabulous job right out of college with an international accounting firm, where he made great money and led "the good life." He eventually developed a liking for cocaine, which became a habit he could easily afford initially. Eventually, however, he began dealing to further subsidize his drug use, and he was eventually arrested and convicted on federal drug charges. As a consequence, David served three years in a federal prison, where he did some major soul-searching and confronted his demons. He made a decision to help others who found themselves in similar circumstances and began reaching out to other addicts who needed help. After he served his time and was released from prison, he moved into a group home for recovering addicts and eventually got on the board of directors for the home's national organization.

I listened intently. By the end of his story, I was nearly moved to tears. The honesty, strength of character, and courage he had demonstrated were remarkable. It made him stand out as a special person in my mind, despite his criminal record. I was flattered that he trusted me with his story. I joked that I wouldn't be "advertising" the fact that I was working with convicted felons but felt sure that there could be a woman out there who would be open to meeting him, despite his troubled past.

Meanwhile, I got a call from an old friend who told me that his wife's cousin, Jenny, was moving to DC and asked me to connect with her. Jenny was in her late thirties and had had a difficult divorce. She was planning to move to my area with her infant daughter to live with her parents in Potomac, Maryland. I readily agreed and told them to have Jenny call me. About a month later, a beautiful blonde woman about my own age, holding a baby girl in her arms, arrived on my doorstep. We instantly clicked.

Jenny shared her story with me. She'd worked for a marketing firm in LA and had gotten involved with Chris, a coworker in her office. They married and moved to San Diego together when Chris received a more lucrative offer. Seven years into their marriage after trying for several years, Jenny got pregnant. During what was a difficult pregnancy, Chris got involved with another woman and left Jenny late in her pregnancy. She gave birth alone and couldn't imagine remaining in California anywhere near Chris, so she pulled up stakes and moved back east to her parents' house in Potomac, where they could help support her financially and help raise their new grandchild.

Jenny and I began hanging out regularly, since we had babies the same age. We also discovered that we'd had mutual friends in common from her high school in New York, friends whom I had gone to sleepaway camp with for many years and who had mentioned a girl with her maiden name. It seemed like our friendship had been fated.

With my encouragement, Jenny began trying to date again. I would watch her daughter frequently to free her parents up from babysitting duty. She would often come back from her dates and complain that while it was good to get out, she found most of the men who asked her out to be "nerdy and boring."

The inspiration to introduce her to David hit me during one of those venting sessions. "Well, if you want to meet someone interesting, I know a guy who's done time," I said. I knew he'd be attracted to her, and I sensed that she'd think he was cute and would appreciate his intellect and humor. I also suspected that their respective traumas could be a bonding force between them.

"Some of my best friends have done time," she joked and then asked about his circumstances. After I explained further and recommended him so highly, she was intrigued and said she'd be open to meeting him.

Yet I understood that David would have a problem being introduced to a single mom. Although he'd expressed a desire to have a family "someday," he was in no financial position to consider it at the time. I had to approach this carefully.

I picked up the phone and called David.

"Please humor me here, David. I have a new friend who just moved here from LA under difficult circumstances. She has a baby and isn't in a position to get out very often. She doesn't know anyone and hasn't really explored the area at all. Would you be willing to meet her and see if perhaps you could introduce her around to some nice people?"

David paused. "Sure," he responded with a reluctance that came through loud and clear.

I knew he probably felt beholden to me for having listened to his story without judgment and thought he should repay my kindness. To my relief, he agreed to meet her. By now, I had really bonded with Jenny and desperately wanted to see her with a decent man. I thought highly enough of David to believe that he was one of the "good guys" out there, despite his past, and was delighted that he was onboard, even though I could sense that he wasn't thrilled with the idea.

I looked at this "match" purely as an experiment. Jenny and David would be the first couple introduced through my matchmaking practice, even though I hadn't yet begun to charge fees at that time. After some back and forth, they eventually made plans to meet in downtown DC for dinner the following Saturday night. The next morning, Jenny called unusually early to "report in."

I was delighted to hear from her and asked, "So how did it go?"

Jenny responded, "Leora, forget law. You have found your calling!"

"Really," I asked. "I guess it went well?"

"Let's put it this way," she continued. "We ended up kissing on the steps of the Lincoln Memorial until 1:00 a.m. I've never had a better first date. We're absolutely smitten!"

This was all the validation I needed to move forward with my business plan. I was happy that I'd listened to my instincts and "thought out of the box" to make that first match, which to David's surprise, turned out to be a "home run." David and Jenny indeed fell in love that first night. Shortly thereafter, to her parents' amazement and over their objections, Jenny and her daughter moved in with David. About six months later, they were married. David adopted Jenny's daughter, who had essentially been abandoned by her biological father. Three years later, they had a second daughter together. David and Jenny ended up being the unlikely poster couple for my matchmaking service. They have expressed their gratitude over the years through frequent media interviews, always giving me mad props for the life-altering decision I made to introduce them to each other.

## CHAPTER FIFTEEN

# Physician, Heal Thyself

From its inception, I ran my matchmaking business from home. The flexibility of a home-based business worked well with my responsibilities as a mother to a toddler and an infant at the time. I continued to eagerly build the business by meeting with potential clients, circulating in the community to market my company, and developing relationships with strategic partners who were in a position to send me referrals. This involved a tremendous amount of time and energy and began to take on a life of its own. At that time, Howard worked full time as an attorney for the federal government.

Howard and I began to function like "ships in the night." I had part-time childcare for my children, but I continued to work and take care of the kids during the day. Most evenings, when Howard came home, I'd have evening appointments or events to attend. I also worked most weekends and set aside one full day to meet potential clients who weren't available to meet during the week. Momentum for my business grew, and I was determined to take advantage of every opportunity that came my way. In the excitement, I failed to notice Howard becoming increasingly unhappy with my absence or his desire for more family time together. I presumed that since he had supported the idea of my starting the business, he understood what it would mean in terms of my time commitment to such an endeavor. After all, I reasoned, I had supported him during his professional transition from private to government practice as a lawyer, even though that process involved a significant financial sacrifice for our family. I thought it only fair that my ambitions be taken equally as seriously.

Perhaps if I had paid more attention to Howard's feelings, I would have understood that he was unhappy with our situation, but I was completely caught up in the excitement of a new business and on a mission to establish myself. The differences in our personalities surfaced as we tried to navigate this process. I didn't respond to Howard's subtle messages, since my own communication style is much more direct. He didn't ask for changes to be made, so I presumed that he was fully accepting of our situation. Instead, an undercurrent of resentment began to build, and with it, the unraveling of our marriage at the exact time I began to experience success as a matchmaker and "expert" in relationships. The irony was not lost on me.

Then a crisis shook the very foundation of our family life. At eighteen months old, our son was diagnosed with autism. Shortly after Adam's first birthday, right around the time he began to learn to walk, we started to notice Adam begin to retreat into himself and fail to respond to cues or make eye contact with us. When we were out in public, he would run aimlessly and fail to respond to his name being called as he had before. This problem peaked on a family vacation that turned out to be a nightmare. Howard and I spent the entire time chasing after Adam and trying in vain to get him to engage with us.

Upon our return home, we consulted one of the top experts in the field, who evaluated Adam and informed us that we were facing a very serious problem. He advised us that in order to prevent Adam from regressing any further developmentally, Howard and I would need to go "all out." This meant providing Adam with a team of therapists who would begin a weekly treatment regimen consisting of play therapy, occupational therapy, and speech therapy. We were devastated and overwhelmed.

With the financial support of both our families, we went into "emergency mode" and accessed the finest therapists in the area. The stress on us was tremendous, and the differences in our personalities and problem-solving skills surfaced with a vengeance. While I mourned the loss of my "typical" child, I accepted this new reality with a determination to give my son everything he needed. I didn't think that I needed to sacrifice my own career ambitions to accomplish this, especially since I was only working part-time and was mostly home during the day. Howard, on the other hand, felt that my unwillingness to be a full-time caretaker to our son would jeopardize Adam's progress. He resolved to step up and do so himself, despite my presence in the home during the day. Over my objections, Howard took a six-month leave of absence from his job as a government attorney to stay home and manage Adam's "recovery," as he saw it.

Our marriage began to deteriorate even further once Howard took his leave of absence from work. He seemed hell-bent on finding a cure for Adam, while I struggled to accept Adam's diagnosis and work with it as best as I could. Our daughter, Elana, who was about five years old at the time, was a precocious and sweet little girl, who was comparatively easy to care for. Nonetheless, she still required and deserved considerable attention herself, which we were both committed to providing. The stress of our home life was onerous, but, sadly, we were unable to find comfort and understanding in each other. Instead, our differences drove us further apart.

After six months of having Howard at home, I found the situation to be intolerable. I told Howard that it was unnecessary for him to continue to be home full time and that our finances required him to go back to work. He was reluctant to do so and felt that Adam would not get the care he needed if left to me and part-time babysitters. I experienced Howard's lack of trust in me as a mother as a major blow. It felt as if he blamed me for our son's condition. He had been the first to identify Adam's issues and now felt vindicated and indispensable to Adam's recovery. I disagreed.

Howard reluctantly agreed to return to work on the condition that I would allow his parents, who were newly retired and living in Pittsburgh, to move to our area and become Adam's caregivers while I worked. I wasn't crazy about the idea but consented to his terms with one stipulation: they rent their own apartment nearby and not live with us full time. They agreed and signed a six-month lease on an apartment in downtown Bethesda.

Within a short period of time, I began to feel like a stranger in my own home. My in-laws, who meant well and only wanted to help, had their own ideas about how our household should be run and essentially took over. While I appreciated their help, I experienced it as overly intrusive. I felt outnumbered, overwhelmed, and depressed over my home life, which prompted me to work even harder in my business to avoid being home much.

I was relieved when the six months ended and Howard returned to work. Unfortunately, Howard felt overwhelmed himself. Rather than ask for help, he desperately continued to try find a cure for our son. In addition to the special education and intensive therapy Adam was receiving, Howard insisted that we try various diets and alternative treatments, all of which were expensive, time consuming, and ultimately futile. This pattern continued for the next several years, as I struggled to be the best mother I knew how, build my business, and salvage our rapidly unraveling marriage.

I was at my wit's end. As a result, I insisted on couple's therapy. Howard reluctantly granted my request, but after seeing three different couple's counselors, we were unable to resolve our problems. Eventually, I began working with my own therapist to handle my anger, frustration, and depression over our failing marriage. I asked Howard to move out of our bedroom, and he obliged. He moved downstairs into our spare bedroom, which had previously served as a guest room. We lived that way for the next year.

I hesitantly began a course of antidepressant medication, at my therapist's urging. I was surprised at how much better I began to feel. Soon, I became more like my old self. My confidence and strength gradually returned, and I began to consider the idea of leaving my marriage. I had resisted taking that step for several years due to my desire to see Adam further along before risking any potential harm to him by breaking up the family. Eventually, however, the atmosphere in the house became increasingly toxic. With the help of my therapist and support from family and friends, I realized that I needed to get out of my marriage and move on. My mental health and that of my children's were at stake. Also, my integrity and credibility as a professional matchmaker required me to finally admit that my own marriage had reached its end.

I was terrified to separate from Howard for fear that my reputation as a matchmaker would be tarnished once it became public. I had, by then, been working for years to build my business by not only serving clients but also giving presentations and workshops on how to build and maintain loving relationships. Clients had looked up to me as a role model, as a successful wife, mother, and professional to be emulated. But with the support of an excellent therapist, I was able to work on the voice in my head that plagued me. My mother had drummed into me the "What will people say?" mentality. She, like most women of her generation, was perpetually concerned about "appearances."

As I delved deeper into therapy, I came to understand that
my parents, who I knew deep down were not well matched, had
stayed together due to their own histories of survival and their
concerns for their children and how others would see them if they
divorced. They were also a product of their time, which frowned
upon divorce. In a true "light bulb" moment, I realized that I had
probably become a matchmaker to reconcile the pain I felt as the
child of two loving but romantically incompatible parents. I knew
instinctively, even then, that despite their best efforts to appear
otherwise, each of them would have been much happier had they
chosen different partners in life.

Howard and I separated in the spring of 1993. I was terrified, but
to my surprise and relief, becoming single didn't hurt my business
at all. In fact, it miraculously flourished. I wondered whether it
was because the burden of my troubled marriage had been lifted
so I could be truly authentic with people once again. Or perhaps it
was because my clients now recognized that I not only empathized
with their circumstances but now lived a similar lifestyle myself.
I also found that, as a single woman, I was invited to many more
singles' events, which enabled me to network more effectively than
I had while married. Whatever the reasons, I was grateful that my
business could support me during this major life transition.

The divorce took three years to finalize. There was a brief period
when Howard and I tried again, but we were unable to reconnect
to the feelings that brought us together in the first place. So much
water under the bridge had driven an emotional wedge between us
that was impossible to traverse.

Then our legal struggles began. Divorcing another attorney made
the process even more challenging than it needed to be. During
those three years, despite the stressors and ups and downs of the
divorce process, I began to gather my strength and return to the
person I had been before my marital problems began. I learned
that by putting my energy into helping my clients, I experienced a

level of healing that I might not have achieved without that focus in my life. I became better at my work, as I now lived the pain that my divorced clients had been through. As a result, I developed a deeper capacity for empathy and love toward those who came to me for help in finding new, healthier relationships.

Once I became single, the boundaries between my personal and professional lives had the potential to become blurred. As a married matchmaker, this was a nonissue, but from the time Howard and I separated, I resolved to reestablish myself as a serious professional. There were no rules of ethics in the matchmaking profession, as there had been in my legal practice, so I established my own. I made it clear to my members and the public that as a policy, I would not date my clients, nor would I work with men whom I had dated.

My business, of course, involved many singles' events and parties. I was perfectly free to meet anyone I wanted personally, as long as I didn't enter into a business relationship with them. This became confusing and stressful at times. Often, I walked into an event asking myself whether I should wear my "matchmaker" or my "Leora" hat that night. When I would decide to go the "Leora" route and things didn't play out the way I had hoped, I would berate myself for wasting a business opportunity. I would then console myself by saying, "I'm only human" and "My desire to meet someone special is perfectly normal and not a waste of time." This internal battle persisted the entire time I was single.

During that time, two of my members tested my policy on not dating my clients and boldly asked me out once they learned that I was single again. Truth be told, had I truly wanted either of them for myself, my ethics might not have stood up. Thankfully, that wasn't the case with either of them.

I had been working with Ken for about a year. He was a handsome entrepreneur who was considerably older than me, divorced, with no children. I felt extremely flattered by his interest, since he was highly picky, but I also understood that we were not well-suited for each other. Ken had many appealing qualities: he was Jewish, from New York, had a very masculine presence, and a fabulous sense of humor. My conversations with him were always thought provoking and entertaining. I could sense that he found me attractive even before I became single, but once he actually acknowledged his attraction to me, I thought it best to nip it in the bud. "I'm flattered, Ken," I told him, "but I think it's best to maintain our business relationship. Besides, I don't think I'm what you need in a mate, and I'm still committed to finding you that right person. Thank you for the compliment, though." He was gracious enough to accept my diplomatically worded rejection.

The same scenario played itself out with Ted, an architect in his early forties who had never married and was seeking a wife and a family. I was surprised when Ted asked me out, since I knew he wanted to have his own children, and I had two of my own and wasn't having any more. I asked myself whether his interest in me might be a result of the professional intimacy we had developed between us, not unlike the transference that might occur between a therapist and their patient. Whatever the reasons, I understood that dating Ted would be a mistake. He was awfully cute, though. Perhaps, if I had met him in a different context, I might have been open to him, but I was clear that since we were in a business relationship, we needed to keep it there. I told him that while I was flattered, I didn't think it was a good idea to mix business with my personal life. He said he understood and thanked me for my integrity.

As it turned out, I introduced both Ken and Ted to their future wives. I recommended Ken to Sharon, an attractive lawyer in her midforties, who had grown tired of the corporate life and yearned for a quieter existence. She and Ken hit it off, married, and moved out of the Washington, DC, area and settled down in North Carolina, where he ran his businesses from home and she began a consulting practice. I referred Ted to Nancy, a woman in her late thirties who, like him, was interested in marriage and a family. They married a year later and had a beautiful wedding in her hometown of Boston, complete with cherry blossom centerpieces. They went on to have two beautiful children, whom they are happily raising in Bethesda, Maryland.

My instincts to stay out of the mix were right in both cases. I felt gratified that my common sense prevailed and that I succeeded for Ken and Ted. Surprisingly, however, sometimes the reverse happened, as in the case with Chad. I had met him at a singles' boating event in Baltimore, sponsored by a colleague who had encouraged me to attend. Chad was, in my opinion, the epitome of the perfect male specimen. He was tall, had a full head of sandy blond hair, twinkling green eyes, a phenomenal physique from a strict exercise regimen, and an enchanting smile. When he approached and engaged me in conversation, I actually found myself getting weak at the knees. He was intelligent and sweet, and although we came from entirely different backgrounds, when he asked me out, I was thrilled.

Our first date consisted of dinner and a movie in downtown DC. After the movie, we went to a nearby restaurant where I ran into Roz, one of my fairly new clients about my age. As Chad and I walked past her on our way to be seated, I gave Roz a subtle nod, not wanting to intrude or violate confidentiality by revealing her as a client to the group of women at her table.

The next morning, I received an e-mail from Roz accusing me of "stealing all the good men for myself." I was stunned. I wrote back explaining to her that Chad was not a client and that my personal life was irrelevant to our working relationship. Unfortunately, and not surprisingly, Roz was one of the clients for whom I didn't succeed. I found her difficult to please as a client and her personality to be quite abrasive. Things with Chad never went anywhere either. I marveled at how complicated being a single matchmaker was.

## CHAPTER SIXTEEN

# A Psychic's Prediction

$A$ nnabelle was a beautiful, olive-skinned, petite brunette in her forties with a heavy French accent. While she dressed stylishly, her clothes appeared to be somewhat dated, as if purchased secondhand. Annabelle approached me shyly after my presentation to a group of singles in a Silver Spring, Maryland, home in late October of 1990. She pulled me aside and whispered, "Leora, I have to tell you something. I have psychics in my family, and I know you're going to find me my husband." I had no idea how to respond, so I let her continue. "All I want is to make a man happy," she stated.

"Who says that kind of thing anymore?" I thought. I immediately assumed she might be crazy, or a relic of the past, but couldn't quite tell just yet.

Annabelle proceeded to tell me her story. A Sephardic Jewish woman, born and raised in Cairo, Egypt, she had been married at age nineteen, which was customary in her culture. It wasn't exactly an arranged marriage, but it had the endorsement of both influential Jewish families within their community. She and her husband had a daughter, Claire, early on in their marriage. From that point on, the verbal and emotional abuse began, which eventually led to regular physical assaults. When things got so bad that Annabelle began to fear for her daughter's safety, she made the monumental decision to leave. With her family's approval, she fled with her daughter to Belgium, where her older brother lived and took them in. They lived in Brussels for ten years before moving to the United States.

Annabelle and Claire, who was thirteen years old at the time, settled in Montgomery County, Maryland. Annabelle got an administrative job in local government, which barely supported them. After a substantial waiting period, she became eligible for subsidized housing in Bethesda in a much safer neighborhood than where they had been living. Annabelle had only a high school education, and she was determined to better herself in her new country. She enrolled in evening classes in early childhood development and eventually earned a degree in the field. She also took babysitting jobs whenever she could to supplement her meager government salary.

Annabelle had a deep love for Judaism and worshipped at a few different Orthodox synagogues in the Maryland suburbs. At each synagogue, she would ask the rabbi whether he knew of any eligible single men whom she could meet. She was repeatedly disappointed at their seeming indifference in helping her in this area of her life.

Touched by Annabelle's story, I warmed to her immediately. I concluded that she was not only sane but also highly evolved spiritually, even if she held on to old-world traditions. She wanted my help as a matchmaker, and I knew men would find her desirable. After learning of her circumstances, however, I told her that I didn't think it would be appropriate for me to represent her because, as I understood it, she couldn't afford my fees. In response, Annabelle offered to barter with me by babysitting for my children in exchange for introductions to eligible men. I liked her enough to consider trying this arrangement and invited her over to meet my family. My children, ages four and one at the time, were immediately drawn to her loving and playful nature. She came laden with a huge plate of crêpes suzettes still warm from her kitchen, and they gobbled them up eagerly, to her delight. After that, she brought them over every time she watched them. Very soon, she became like a member of the family.

Shortly thereafter, I introduced Annabelle to a very successful entrepreneur in the area who thought she was pretty but "too out of touch" with American culture. Meanwhile, she met other men on her own through personal ads, a pre-Internet way for singles to meet at that time. The process involved placing or responding to classified ads in popular magazines for one's personal life rather than career. Annabelle was only partly successful with the personals. The men she met were happy to take her to bed, but, unfortunately for Annabelle, they weren't interested in a committed relationship, for whatever reason.

Years passed. Annabelle and I became good friends. My children loved her like an "honorary aunt." One day, I got a call from a therapist in Baltimore who was familiar with my work. She informed me that she was working with a very special fifty-two-year-old single man named Harvey who was inexperienced with women and wondered if I knew anyone who would be open to meeting him. She went on to explain how Harvey had been raised by a very difficult mother and a toxic sister and thus avoided relationships with women, even though he was attracted to them. She described him as a "really good guy" who was ready to move forward in this area of his life. Plus, he was well situated financially and could offer the right woman a very comfortable lifestyle.

I immediately thought of Annabelle. In her midforties, she'd been married and in a few relationships since then and could therefore "show him the ropes" sexually. Plus, she was a sweetheart and could make a man feel very safe. And while someone's financial support would be a major blessing for her, she wouldn't be in it for the money but, rather, for the love she understandably craved.

I was right. Their chemistry was immediate, but their courtship was slow and steady. Harvey lived in New Jersey, so the distance prevented them from spending too much time together at first. Given Annabelle's job and responsibilities toward Claire, who had become a challenging teenager by then, their time together was limited. Harvey was patient, however, and Annabelle was thrilled about their budding romance. With a gleam in her eye and a charming French accent, she confided to me that she was teaching him all about "ze passionate kiss."

Nine months later, I was honored to stand alongside Annabelle and Harvey under their wedding canopy at a local synagogue. Annabelle looked elegant and radiant in her Chanel cream silk wedding suit. On that sunny February afternoon, her diamond ring sparkled in the light streaming through the stained glass windows. It was Valentine's Day, 1993.

## CHAPTER SEVENTEEN

# Absence Makes the Heart Grow Fonder

*I*n the ten years since my last evening with Ian in London, I couldn't get him out of my mind. Our time together had been enchanting and so tempting! I had often daydreamed about what life would have been like had I stayed in London and gotten involved with him. I cherished the silver bracelet he had given me as a parting gift, and I wore it often as a reminder of my most hopeful days, especially when things weren't going well with Howard.

There was no way of actually knowing what would have been had I made the decision to remain there and become qualified to practice law there, but I had all the ingredients in place to have made a life for myself in London. I had worked for a prestigious criminal law firm, where I was liked and well respected. I had three roommates who were close to my own age and had become very good friends. Plus, I had my family there, whom I adored. Between my two uncles, two aunts, and four cousins, I would have had a family support system to sustain me, unlike my situation in Washington, DC, where I had no family and had to make friends from scratch. I told myself that I had no reason to dwell on such thoughts, since I had decided long ago not to take that path in life, and there would be no going back on those choices.

There I was, separated from Howard and facing a daunting journey ahead. I decided to visit my family in London for a long weekend, which I tended to do at least once a year. This time, their support would be timely and therapeutic.

I arrived on a Thursday and stayed with Hertel and Gerhard, who, as always, treated me like royalty. That Friday, on a whim, I decided to see if I could track down Ian through the phone numbers I had kept over the past ten years. To my disappointment, they had all been disconnected. I was not to be deterred, however. I contacted Jill, my old friend from Prisoner's Abroad. After reminiscing and making plans to meet for a drink that Sunday evening before my departure on Monday, I asked her whether she had a way to get a hold of Ian. She gave me his mother's phone number in Cornwall, England, and wished me luck tracking him down.

I took a deep breath and called the number. An elderly woman with a strong English accent answered. I introduced myself as an old friend of Ian's from America and asked whether she would be kind enough to give me his current contact information. She was happy to help and graciously gave me several numbers to try, explaining that he now divided his time between his home, shop, and a third business.

With my heart in my throat, I called the first number and, surprisingly, got him on the phone right away. After I nervously identifyed myself, he excitedly greeted me. "I don't remember many chats," he said in his charming English accent, "but I certainly remember ours. How long has it been?" he asked.

"Ten years," I responded.

"Amazing," he said. "You sound exactly the same."

Encouraged by his remarks, I explained that I was in town for only a long weekend and asked if he might have any time to get together.

"What a shame," he said. "I wish I had known you were coming. My weekend is already booked. I manage a rock band, and they're having a gig in Epsom, Surrey, this weekend, which I'll be tied up with."

"Really?" I ventured. "Will you be there with anyone?"

"No," he said. "I'm there to work."

"I love rock music," I boldly responded, "and would love to hear your band."

He hesitated. "Well, it's rather far for you. You'd have to take a British Rail train to get there, and the band plays till awfully late."

"No problem," I responded. "I know my way around the transit system here. Besides, I'm leaving on Monday, so this is the only chance I'll have to see you. It's been too long," I persisted.

"Well, if you don't mind watching me work, you're welcome," he said unconvincingly.

"Great," I said, before he had the chance to retract the invitation. "Just give me the details and I'll be there."

As I prepared to hang up, he quickly added, "There's just one thing I need to tell you. I've gone fat and bald."

"Ha ha," I responded, thinking that he was kidding. Ian had been a tall, rather slim fellow, with a full head of hair ten years earlier. I could not imagine that he was being serious. "Thanks for the full disclosure," I teased back.

The trip to Epsom took much longer than I had anticipated. I took the Underground from North London to Victoria Station in South London, and from there I waited for a British Rail train to Epsom. The journey took almost three hours.

I got off the train and studied the street map at the station to figure out how to get to the concert hall. It turned out to be much further than it looked on the map. After walking for a half hour in the chilly darkness, I wasn't sure whether or not I was headed in the right direction, so I stepped into a pub to inquire.

"Hello, love! How can I help?" the bartender asked.

I asked him how I could find the Charles Theatre, and he quickly directed me to the right place.

"You're a long way from home," he said. "Be careful, love!"

By the time I got to the concert hall, my heart was beating wildly, not only from having walked so fast but also in anticipation of seeing Ian again. "This is silly," I told myself. "For all you know, Ian could be married with a couple of kids by now, or at least have a girlfriend." I snuffed out that inner voice and walked into the main entrance, trying to smooth out my curly hair, which had turned into a mess from the blustery walk from the train station. By then, it was close to 9:00 p.m.

I told the ticket taker that I was there to see Ian, and he asked me to wait as they called him from backstage. When he appeared, I was taken aback. He had indeed been honest with me about his looks, and I had to adjust to this "new Ian" in front of me. Despite his weight gain and hair loss, however, I still found myself drawn to him. Upon seeing me, he gave me a wide grin and invited me to have a drink with him at the bar upfront.

His energy was magnetic. It felt as if no time had passed between us. Ian explained that he had to head backstage shortly but had arranged a spot for me to observe the concert from the sound booth. In the twenty minutes we sat together, I learned, to my tremendous relief, that he was, in fact, single. He explained that after running around for several years, he'd had a serious girlfriend who had tragically died of ovarian cancer at age thirty-one. He'd been alone ever since. My heart went out to him. I shared the highlights of my own saga with him and proudly showed him photos of my children. Shortly afterward, Ian was called backstage. He escorted me to the sound booth where he had arranged a comfortable chair for me and said he'd join up with me after the performance.

Concerned about my making it back to London safely after the performance, Ian offered me a ride with his friend, who owned a taxi service and would make sure to get me to an Underground station at whatever time I needed, since British Rail stopped running after 1:00 a.m. on weekends. While I appreciated his concern for my well-being, I was uncharacteristically unconcerned about those details, especially since, prior to my departure from London, I had already informed my aunt that I might be home very late and not to wait up. I was totally living in the moment.

I sat in the sound booth sipping white wine while watching Ian work as the band manager. He made sure the equipment was working properly and did a sound check on each mic as the band set up. By the time the music played, I had a nice wine buzz going and began to move to the music. I marveled at his confidence and stage presence as he maneuvered around the band members and saw to all the details. I found myself more and more impressed as I sat there staring at him. He was in total command of the evening and seemed to be completely comfortable in his own skin. As the evening wore on, I became mesmerized by him and made a decision then and there that whatever it took, he would be mine.

The band played until midnight, at which time Ian had to help pack up the equipment. I waited patiently for him to finish as I chatted with some of his friends. When he was done, he suggested we go somewhere for a bite to eat. I eagerly agreed, since I hadn't eaten dinner and needed something to help soak up the wine I'd been drinking all evening.

The only place open in the small suburb at that hour was the local Pizza Hut. I didn't really eat pizza but couldn't have cared less where we went. I just took his lead. We drove there in his van, parked, and found a booth in the restaurant, which we occupied until everyone else had left and the place was about to close. We talked about everything that had transpired over the preceding ten years, sharing intimate details with each other with remarkable ease. As Ian gazed at me intently with his piercing blue eyes, I lost all sense of time and place and felt myself falling deeper and deeper under his spell. When the lights began to flicker, Ian put down some cash, took my hand, and led me back to his van. I didn't ask where we were going or whether he had arranged a ride for me with his friend, as we had discussed. I just followed him blindly.

We sat in silence as Ian drove for about twenty minutes through the vacant streets of Epsom. Finally, he pulled up in front of what I presumed was his home, a modest two-story brick row house, and invited me in. I was surprised to see another man, who turned out to be his roommate, Martin, watching TV in the living room. Ian introduced us, and the three of us shared a brandy and some laughs together. Then Martin, tactfully excused himself and went upstairs.

Ian and I remained on the couch and discussed the fact that it made no sense for me to try to get back to London, since it was already about 2:00 a.m. I agreed. He then took my hand, and, when I didn't pull back, leaned in for a kiss. I eagerly responded. Ian's kiss was sensuous, yet urgent. He moved on top of me on the couch, and we continued to kiss passionately. Then, in the most nonchalant manner, he got up, took my hand, and said, "Come to bed," as if we'd been a couple for years.

I followed him upstairs, knowing there was no turning back. I hadn't been with anyone but Howard for the last ten years, so I was nervous and self-conscious. Once we entered his bedroom, however, my inhibitions disappeared. Our clothes seemed to dissolve as our bodies melded together with reckless abandon. I felt a level of passion that I had never experienced before. Ten years of longing had finally been fulfilled. The chemistry between us was instantaneous and felt totally natural. It was a magical night.

When I woke up the next morning next to Ian, it all came flooding back. I thought I had dreamt the whole thing, but there he was. Reality hit me, and I realized that I needed to get myself together and back to London before my family began to seriously worry about me. I frantically threw on my clothes while Ian began to get organized to drive me to the train station. There was no time to linger.

As I waited for Ian to come out of the bathroom, a tremendous wave of sadness hit me when I contemplated leaving him. I began to cry. Embarrassed by my display of emotion, I quickly pulled myself together and put on a brave face as Ian emerged. He ushered me out of the house and into his van. I asked him to convey my goodbyes to Mark, who had been nice enough to give us our privacy.

Once in his van again, we held hands and said very little as we drove along. I silently prayed for the drive to take as long as possible. Neither of us said anything about seeing each other again, understanding that our night together had been practically other-worldly and impossible to define. When he pulled up to the station, I thanked him for everything, kissed him quickly on the cheek, and exited his van, making a point not to look back.

When I returned to London, I couldn't help but confide in Aunt Hertel about the previous night's events. I was so fortunate to have had an aunt like her. She was a passionate woman herself, full of life, empathy, and entirely without judgment. She knew what I had been through with Howard and was actually happy about this turn of events with Ian, although she cautioned me to try to keep my feelings under control. After all, she reasoned, it was only one night and might not amount to anything more. What she said made sense, but in my heart, I felt as if a seismic shift had taken place, the significance of which I'd only learn over time.

That evening, I got together with Jill and told her that thanks to her, I'd actually seen Ian on Saturday at his gig in Surrey and he sent his regards. I did not tell her that we'd been intimate and that I'd ended up staying the night, since I wanted to protect Ian's privacy as well as my own. I mused over the irony of the situation. Ten years ago, she and Gregg had tried their hand at matchmaking when they had asked us to represent the organization at that fundraiser together. They had apparently seen something between us that neither Ian nor I could see at the time, but things hadn't gone anywhere back then due to my engagement to Howard. I had felt as though I would be cheating to even entertain the idea of seeing anyone else and had made sure that things between us remained platonic. Now, the genie had been let out of the bottle, in all its splendor.

My flight home was turbulent, literally and figuratively. When I looked back at the events from that Saturday night, it all felt surreal. Had all of that really happened? My mind struggled to grasp it, while my body reminded me that it had. Details of being with Ian came flooding back, sending tingling sensations throughout my body. I felt an inexplicable happiness, even though I knew that we lived a continent apart. "Be grateful for the experience," I told myself. "This should serve as a sign that magic can still happen, and leave it at that."

But I couldn't stop thinking about him. I returned to my life at home: my children, the stress of the looming divorce, the pressure of building my business, and my son's condition. Shortly after, I received another blow. My mother was diagnosed with metastatic colon cancer. The bottom seemed to fall out of my life at that point. She had been my best friend, the rock on which I had relied my entire life. I was crushed with the realization that while I knew she would put up a fight all the way, her days were ultimately numbered.

I wrote Ian immediately (an actual letter, in the days before e-mail) and thanked him for a night I'd never forget. I also shared the latest turn of events. He wrote back, in gorgeous cursive penmanship, expressing his feelings that our night together had been one of the highlights of his entire life. I knew he wasn't the sort of fellow who made such statements lightly. As I read his words, I felt my heart skip a beat. It appeared that it wasn't just a one-night stand for him either. Something major had stirred in him as well. A romantic crack in his armor had opened up for him for the first time in a very long time.

Ian and I began corresponding regularly. In his letters, he expressed his passion for me in erotic detail worthy of a best-selling adult novel. That, coupled with his empathy and friendship, served as a welcome buffer to the harsh realities I faced on a daily basis. The letters took on a life of their own, and I anticipated their arrival like an addict waiting for the next fix. Ian became obsessed with writing to me as well and would often stay up into the wee hours of the night, his thoughts racing as he composed his masterpieces. They were each at least ten pages long, always handwritten. In between, he'd send romantic little gifts, like jewelry or a beautiful piece of crystal. I became smitten with him from the letters alone. The energy between us was symbiotic.

During the initial phase of our correspondence, I dreamt that I was a figure skater in full costume on an enormous, empty ice-skating rink, circling, soaring, and twirling about like an Olympic champion, my auburn curls flying in the breeze. When I awoke, I felt a sense of overwhelming joy. "Where did that come from?" I asked myself. I had been a skater as a child but hadn't been on the ice for decades. I marveled at the complicated workings of the subconscious.

I had to share my dream with Ian right away, so I called him the next day. Neither of us had spoken to each other since that fateful night together. Our communication had been limited to our letters, as if we were laying a written foundation for our budding relationship. In them, we were able to share our innermost thoughts, feelings, and dreams with each other before even considering where this would all lead. But, I could no longer resist my need to speak to him.

When I got him on the phone, the mere sound of his voice sent a physical charge through me. "I love you," he stated. "I loved you from that first night. I don't know how this happened, but I can't stop thinking about you and wanting you," he said.

I was elated. "I love you too," I confessed with a lump forming in my throat. When can I see you again?"

"As soon as possible," he replied.

I knew from his letters that he had a birthday coming up and suggested I come over so that we could celebrate together. He loved the idea, so I immediately set about booking a flight and making arrangements to be there within the next three weeks. My plan was to arrive in London and stay with Aunt Hertel for a night before heading south to Surrey for the rest of the weekend.

The next three weeks passed agonizingly slowly as I anticipated my reunion with Ian. I obsessed over wanting to look my best for him. I practically threw half of my closet into my suitcase, which was bursting at the seams as I dragged it through the airport. In those days, not all luggage came with built-in wheels, which made the task even more challenging. Rationally, I knew I had gone way overboard, since I was only going for a long weekend, but I couldn't help myself. Even the porter at the airport gave me the "stink eye" as he tried to lift my bag.

I arrived in London on a Thursday and was met at the airport by my uncle Benno, a sweet soul who took pride in always meeting his American family at the airport and then driving us to his sister Hertel's house. They all welcomed me with open arms and were kind and understanding enough not to give me a hard time when I told them of my plans to head south for the rest of the weekend. Aunt Hertel just winked and smiled.

Ian was set to meet me on the train platform in Epsom. Our plan was to go out for a romantic birthday dinner before returning to his house. I took great pains to dress nicely in a clingy sweater and skirt outfit suitable for the chilly October English weather. As my train drew nearer to the station, my heart fluttered wildly. I began to sweat with anticipation. A very nice gentleman on the train offered to help me with my suitcase. He grimaced in surprise when he lifted it once we pulled into the station.

Ian stood there waiting. My heart crept into my throat. The Good Samaritan handed my bag over to Ian, who said, "Cheers, mate!" and then grimaced himself once he lifted my bag. He put it down with a thud and then put his hands on my face and whispered softly into my ear, "You're really here." Then, he wrapped his arms around me for what seemed like an eternity.

When we finally pulled apart and looked at each other, Ian immediately made fun of my suitcase. "What do you have in here, bricks?" he asked.

"I didn't mean to get carried away," I explained. "I just wanted to make sure I had everything I needed."

"Are you moving in?" he chided. "You have enough here for three weeks, not three days."

We laughed as he lifted my suitcase with one arm. I held on to the other as we made our way out of the station.

We had a wonderfully romantic birthday dinner in a posh restaurant of Ian's choosing. Oddly, during the meal, I was facing the window to the street and observed several fellows peering in and talking to one another. When I mentioned it and Ian turned around, he realized that they were his buddies who had come for a glimpse of the American lass who had captured Ian's heart. I was embarrassed but flattered nonetheless. We lingered over the meal, as if it were foreplay, before heading back to his house. His roommate, Martin, had arranged to spend the weekend at his girlfriend's house to give us the privacy he knew we needed.

As it turned out, we ended up not leaving the house for three days. My robe was the only article of clothing I even used, which I slipped in and out of as the days turned to night and the weekend became one long interlude of monumental proportions. We were totally in sync, physically and spiritually.

Occasionally, we'd stop to eat something and snack on the raspberry birthday cake, his favorite flavor, which I had brought with me from London for his forty-first birthday. During one of our "breaks," we decided to have some reading time in bed, and we both pulled out the exact same novel we'd both been reading without the other's knowledge. We had a great laugh over that, along with many other things.

Ian began referring to me as "The Mrs." and told me that it felt to him as if we'd been together for years. When the weekend was over, once again, my heart broke at the thought of saying goodbye. This time, however, I knew this was only the beginning and not the end, so I wasn't devastated, just sad to be leaving for the time being.

When I got back home, it was as if I had formed a built-in shield for all of my problems. Knowing that Ian was there for me emotionally, despite the distance between us, gave me the strength and courage to handle everything that came my way. My mother's illness was a major stressor in my life. Even though she lived in Brooklyn, I did my best to spend as much time with her as I could and to support her through her complicated and agonizing maze of surgeries and treatments.

During one of my visits, I confided in her about Ian. I knew she could relate, since she too had fallen in love with an Englishman, Edward, whom I had met previously. I realized that this was more than coincidence at play. It was as if I had inherited her passion for the English, as well as her attraction to prominent, brilliant men.

Her lover had been a highly regarded journalist for the *London Times*. Ian was a business owner who became a lobbyist in

Parliament and a fundraiser for pro bono legal services in his community. He was highly respected by politicians and judges alike. I admired his values and talent. Perhaps my attraction to Ian was yet another way to identify with my mother, with whom I felt a deep soul connection.

"I love him," I told my mother, "and despite the distance between us, I know he loves me."

She looked at me and wisely said, "Leora'le," her Yiddish term of endearment for me, "he loves you *because* of the distance between you, not in spite of it."

"What a profound statement," I thought. It was just like her to get right to the heart of the matter. She may have been right. But whatever his motives, the love between Ian and me was real, and I reveled in it.

Our relationship deepened as the letters and phone calls continued. He became the best friend I had ever had and made every other relationship, including my marriage, pale by comparison. I was unaware of what I had been missing until Ian. It became the gold standard of relationships.

I had no desire to date anyone locally, although I understood full well that things between Ian and I couldn't last forever. I couldn't leave the country because of my children and my divorce, which had become increasingly messier. He had no interest in leaving England, where he was a star of sorts. He had explained to me from the beginning that he was a "South London boy" and always would be.

While it hurt to hear that, I understood him and didn't pressure him for more. We resolved to be together and enjoy this for as long as we could and promised each other to let the other know when either of us needed to move on. Meanwhile, we got into a pattern of seeing each other approximately every three months, despite the time and expense involved, which neither of us could really afford. We were all in and simply threw caution to the wind to make sure that we got together as often as possible, no matter what else was happening.

In November, 1994, I traveled with my mother to Leipzig, Germany, her birthplace. I called Ian and asked him to meet me in Frankfurt, where we planned to stay for a few days to visit with my mother's childhood friend. "But I need a new roof," he lamented when I pleaded with him to meet me there. "It's either that or Frankfurt."

"I'll cover the hotel, if you can swing the airfare," I pleaded.

I was desperate to see him, given all the emotions I knew that trip would generate. My mother, who was terminally ill at that point, had been invited as a guest of the city, along with other Holocaust survivors her age, to participate in ten days of memorials and commemorations in honor of the anniversary of *Kristallnacht*, when Jewish businesses and synagogues across Germany had been destroyed. My mother was determined to make the trip, despite her fragile health, and I insisted on accompanying her. She finally relented and was actually very relieved to have me along, since things were much harder for her than she had anticipated. My plan was to tend to her but to be with Ian in between. It was fascinating to have them meet for the first and only time.

My mother, who was four feet eleven inches in heels, stood facing Ian, who was a large man and stood just over six feet tall. They chitchatted for a few minutes. I could see how intimidated Ian was by her, something that was unusual for him.

"I don't scare easily," he told me afterward, "but she definitely scared me."

I thought it was hysterical, as well as flattering. It was as if my mom and I had come full circle. I had met her "English flame," and now, fifteen years later, she had met mine.

Over the course of our stay there, I ran between my mom's

room, helping her dress and bathe, and Ian's room, where we gave in to our ever-present hunger for each other. I made my excuses when it came to spending time with my mother's friend, who was puzzled by my absence. My mother covered for me by explaining that I was spending time with an old friend from London who was "not well and needed my support."

Frankfurt was the perfect ending to a trip that was overwhelming for both my mother and me. She came to terms with her German childhood and legacy while also reconciling herself to her impending death. I watched her gradually make peace with the Germans. The dignitaries who sponsored the event were genuinely remorseful for the sins of the prior generation and devoted to paying their respects to the survivors. They not only honored us but also wined and dined us and treated us to theater, opera, and symphony tickets in between the memorial ceremonies.

It was an enormous media event. Photos of my mother and me were prominently featured in the local papers and, to my astonishment, on the front page of the *International Herald Tribune*. I was overwhelmed with emotion myself, grateful to have borne witness to my mother's journey from fear of confronting her past to reconciliation toward the Germans and peace with her terminal illness. Ian's presence during that trip had been the tonic I had needed, and true to form, he met my needs wholeheartedly.

Our relationship took many twists and turns during what turned out to be a three-year love affair. While we met in London most of the time due to my family, Ian flew over to see me twice during our time together. At first, he was embarrassed to tell me that he had a fear of flying and therefore hadn't traveled much by plane. Touched that his feelings for me overcame his phobia, I was determined to show him a good time on this side of the pond.

In the winter of 1993, Ian flew into Baltimore-Washington International Airport on a nonstop flight from Heathrow. I met him at the airport in a hired limousine so that I could fulfill my limo lovemaking fantasy, complete with champagne, music, and a privacy panel, similar to my favorite scene in the Kevin Costner movie *No Way Out*. I was not disappointed. Despite Ian's jet lag, he felt inspired and deftly fulfilled that fantasy, along with many others that week. We stayed at the Hyatt overlooking Baltimore Harbor, where I introduced him to fried shrimp at Phillip's Seafood and nearby Little Italy for Italian food, which was his favorite.

From there, we took a train to New York, where we stayed in midtown Manhattan and enjoyed all that the city had to offer. It was wonderful to be able to do whatever we wanted, whenever we wanted. One night, we stayed in during the dinner hour and then decided to go out to eat at midnight, something that was unheard of in London at that time. I saw the city I had grown up in anew through his eyes, which I found exhilarating.

We returned to Baltimore by train and walked to my car, which I had parked in the hotel garage. To my chagrin, my car wouldn't start since the battery had died because I had left the dashboard light on the entire weekend. After tolerating my tantrum and waiting for AAA to arrive so we could drive back to Bethesda, Ian settled into my apartment with me. We were both in a state of exhaustion. One of the sweetest things about our relationship was how deeply we both slept when we were together.

Ian's second trip over took place a year later. This time, when he arrived, I could sense something had shifted. In the previous few months, he had told me that he had taken in a new roommate after Martin had gotten married. She was a woman named Lisa, whom he knew professionally. She had suddenly lost her housing and needed a place to stay. He made it sound like he was doing her a favor, but my hackles went up after hearing this, but I still encouraged him to make the trip over.

Soon after he arrived, I learned that Ian and Lisa had become lovers, which deflated me completely. We had always made each other a promise to be completely honest about other people. Why hadn't he told me this before so that I could have spared myself this anguish? I was angry and hurt.

Ian reassured me that it wasn't serious and that I was much prettier than she was, so there was really no reason to worry. He tried to show me how much he still cared, but it became obvious that our relationship was different. We did our best to stay in the present and enjoy each other as we always had, yet I felt doubts creeping insidiously into our relationship, which until then had been based on total trust and full disclosure.

I told myself that I shouldn't be upset. After all, I hadn't been completely faithful to Ian either over those three years. There were times when I dated other men with Ian's knowledge and blessing. He realized that he was far away and always accepted whatever I did, as long as I was honest with him. Now I was getting a taste of my own medicine, which was a bitter pill to swallow. Our lovemaking took on a new urgency, as if this would be our "last hurrah."

> **"There's our sunset, darling," he said. I nodded in agreement, not wanting to fully comprehend the import of his words, which turned out to be prophetic.**

As I drove him back to Dulles Airport in the early evening, the skyline was spectacular. We marveled at the orange and purple clouds streaming across the horizon, as we drove west. "There's our sunset, darling," he said. I nodded in agreement, not wanting to fully comprehend the import of his words, which turned out to be prophetic.

We said our goodbyes, which had always been a difficult experience, but this time there was a finality to it that was undeniable. Over the holidays, he didn't call. I knew that he and Lisa were together and understood that he couldn't bring himself to face me. I was furious that after everything we had been to each other, he could abandon me so abruptly during the holidays. I angrily returned the beautiful suede jacket that I was about to send him for Christmas, which he had admired during his last visit.

When I did finally hear from him after New Year's, he began with an excuse about having to care for his sick aunt. I stopped him in his tracks and told him that it was over. He immediately got it and admitted that it was probably for the best. He could now focus on his relationship with Lisa without feeling conflicted. She was much younger than I and could give him children of his own, which he told me she wanted. It would be a good thing for Ian. I was pleased that I had the courage to back away, knowing that remaining in that situation would be torture for me and would be impossible for Ian as well. We both knew this day would come, and there it was.

I wrote him a final letter, expressing my gratitude and love and wishing him well with Lisa. As I wrote, my tears fell onto the pages, which were smudged by the time I had finished. I still sent it, knowing he would understand. When we were together, we had shared our love of music. One of our favorite songs was "Must Have Been Love" by the Swedish rock group Roxette. I quoted a line from that song in my closing paragraph.

Upon receiving my letter, Ian called. He said the letter was "brilliant" and had touched him deeply. He told me that he was so sorry for everything and that he had truly loved me like no other. I knew it was true and resolved to forgive him.

What was the point in holding on to anger toward him when he had made me happier than I'd ever been? Besides, we had both known that there would be an end date at some point. While I wished it had been because *I* had found someone new to build a future with, I didn't begrudge him his happiness. He'd been loyal to me for years. And while every instinct in me wanted to scratch Lisa's eyes out, luckily, my better nature prevailed.

Ian thanked me for "dragging him out of a coffin that he didn't even know he was in." I understood what he meant. Before I came along, he had been totally shut down emotionally due to his prior loss. He was single for years and proud of not needing anyone. Our relationship had changed all that. I was grateful for the acknowledgment and loved him enough that despite the pain of losing him, I wanted him to have someone and be happy. Besides, I told him, I didn't envy her, since I knew better than anyone that he was "no prize." Upon making this assertion, we had our final laugh and cry together.

A year later, Ian invited me to his and Lisa's wedding, but I couldn't bring myself to attend. Clearly, he wanted to keep me in his life in some fashion, but it was still too painful for me, so I politely declined. I had spent almost every night of that year crying inconsolably into my pillow. I had taken my collection of his letters and burned them in my sink, holding a small ceremony to mark the end of the relationship. I had several recurring dreams of showing up on his and Lisa's doorstep and wreaking havoc upon their new marriage. I tried to imagine what Ian would do in that situation. Eventually, the dreams began to subside and I began to heal. When I asked myself whether it had all been worth it, I always came up with a resounding yes. I hadn't anticipated how deep the pain of our parting would be, but I realized that I wouldn't have given up the experience for anything in the world. Given the choice to do it all over again, I would in a heartbeat.

## CHAPTER EIGHTEEN

# First-Date Follies

*M*y matchmaking practice seemed to take on a life of its own. I divided my time between marketing my services, scouting for matches for my clients, and giving presentations to various singles' groups in the area. I found it exhilarating to tap into a gift that I never realized I had.

I often wondered whether, unbeknownst to my parents, an ancestor of mine in Eastern Europe had been a matchmaker and passed down the gene through several generations. Generations ago, matchmaking had been a very noble profession in Eastern Europe. It was a male-dominated profession at the time, unlike the cultural stereotype of Yente from *Fiddler on the Roof*. Wealthy families would seek out the services of a matchmaker to find scholars (a highly valued but not very lucrative career) for their daughters to marry. This would often require matching from village to village, not unlike today's long-distance relationships. Of course, in modern American culture, successful matches are no longer defined as a business arrangement but, rather, a romantic connection based on physical attraction, shared goals, and values.

One of the things that amazed me the most when I first got started in the business was how many clients threw away perfectly good opportunities, even from the first date. Barry was a sweet, introverted, thirty-five-year-old government attorney with a great sense of humor, once you got to know him. I introduced him to Carol, an attractive brunette and a rising star in the PR field. They were scheduled to meet on a Friday night. On Monday morning, Barry called to report in.

"How did it go?" I asked.

"Not particularly well, I'm afraid," he responded.

Crestfallen, I queried further. "How do you know that?" I asked.

"Well, let's put it this way," he said. "After our dinner, I drove her back to her car, which was parked quite a distance away from the restaurant. She turned to me at a red light and said, 'Don't bother pulling up to the curb. I'll jump out right here.' I think that about sums it up."

I was shocked at Carol's lack of manners and couldn't imagine how her time with Barry could have been that distasteful as to warrant such rudeness on her part. I didn't know whether to laugh or cry. My first instinct was to commiserate with Barry by sharing a chuckle with him over that interaction, which we both agreed was material worthy of a comedy routine. We both understood how inappropriate Carol's parting comments were but couldn't help examining his own performance on the date to try to figure out what could have inspired such an extreme reaction. After providing me with a few more details, we both concluded that he didn't do anything wrong at all. Of course, I couldn't really be sure until I spoke to Carol and got her feedback as well, but it seemed that Carol was the one in need of some dating coaching or, at a minimum, lessons in social etiquette.

Disappointed that she might have squandered a wonderful opportunity with Barry, I resolved to have a chat with her about her experience, per my usual practice. When she reported that the date had gone well but that she was just not attracted to Barry, I asked her whether she was open to some coaching on my part. She reluctantly said yes, so I suggested that even if she didn't think someone was a "match," she ought to be more sensitive to the other person's feelings or, at a minimum, be polite when parting ways. She understood that I thought her behavior had fallen short of that standard, but rather than learn from my feedback, she became defensive. I was disappointed that Carol had wasted a "teachable moment" and resolved not to offer her referrals in the future, as she was not an active client, but someone whom I had recruited for Barry.

It has always been important to me that the people whom I introduce treat each other with respect. It is equally as important for them to express kindness, even if they don't turn out to be a match. Alice's story is a good example.

Alice had just broken up with a boyfriend of two years, whom she had met right after separating from her husband of over twenty years. She seemed to be in somewhat of a state of shock when I met her for a consultation. She explained that her boyfriend, whom she met online, had dumped her suddenly after a very happy two years consisting of mind-blowing sex, luxury vacations, and five-star dinners, all at his expense. She was blissfully happy, until it all came crashing down. She was an adorable, petite, fifty-year-old woman looking to replace what she had lost with her boyfriend. I asked her whether she could be open to someone who was a professional but perhaps not as wealthy as her former lover. She hesitated but said that she could be okay with that as long as he was self-supporting.

With this encouragement, I introduced her to Bobby, a very cute, self-employed attorney. After their first date, Bobby called right away with his feedback. He said that while Alice was very attractive physically, this was "not a match." He explained that she talked nonstop about herself, her marriage, her children, the luxury trips she had taken during her marriage, etc. According to him, whenever he interjected something about himself, she would turn the conversation back to herself and never followed up on any of his comments.

Ironically, they had several fundamental things in common, which was, in large part, the reason I introduced them in the first place. They both had legal backgrounds, they both had raised a son and a daughter, and oddly, they both had lost a sibling under tragic circumstances.

I was disappointed to learn that, according to Bobby, Alice came across as so self-absorbed that she didn't show any curiosity whatsoever about *his* life. Contrary to my membership guidelines, she did not provide me with any feedback of her own until I e-mailed her nearly a week after the date, inquiring about her experience with Bobby. She sent a cursory response saying that they "just didn't connect." I wrote back and asked her what exactly she meant, to which she responded, "We had no chemistry." I then asked her whether she was interested in hearing any of his feedback. While she expressed that she was, she never called me to discuss it, as I had requested. I resolved to find Bobby a woman just as attractive as Alice, but equally as giving as he was. Alice, unfortunately, chose to disengage from my program altogether.

**Sometimes couples are quick to "jump ship" over dealbreakers that may or may not come to fruition.**

A lack of empathy isn't the only issue I've come across in my practice. Sometimes couples are quick to "jump ship" over deal breakers that may or may not come to fruition. Mark, a successful Jewish real estate developer in his early fifties living in Richmond, Virginia, fit this scenario perfectly.

He was a tall, nice-looking fellow with warm blue eyes and a trim physique. He had divorced decades earlier and never had children of his own. He hoped to meet a single mom since he was so family-oriented and loved the idea of having a potential stepfamily. Mark had been involved in several long-term relationships since his divorce. He had built himself a beautiful new home complete with all the latest electronics, including a home theater, which he could share with a potential partner or wife. Like many clients of his ilk, he was extremely picky about his partner's looks and would only consider meeting exceptionally attractive women.

I understood his standards and recruited a fabulous attorney named Shelley for him. A Jewish woman in her late forties, living in the DC area, Shelley was divorced with two grown children, whom she was very close with. She was a beautiful, elegant woman with shoulder-length blonde hair, green eyes, and an athletic figure. When Mark saw her photo, he was more than happy to make the three-hour drive from Richmond to meet her. It was worth a try, I reasoned, since Shelley had expressed her wish to settle down with a financially solid man, and she was willing to consider relocating to his area if they were to become seriously involved.

As I eagerly awaited his feedback after their first date, I gauged the probability of success for this match to be very high. They were both Jewish, attractive, successful, and motivated, having resolved to make whatever adjustments were necessary to make a relationship work.

Mark called the following day and said, "Well, I honestly don't know what to make of this situation. I've never encountered an issue like this before. We were having a great time," he continued. "We seemed to hit it off right away and were chatting over dinner when the subject of funerals came up for some reason. I'm not sure why she even brought up the subject, but she mentioned that she had recently decided that she wanted to be cremated. I was stunned. First of all, she was raised in a Conservative Jewish household, so I was really taken aback that a Jewish person would stray from the traditional Jewish burial practices. As for me, I've already reserved a burial plot for myself. I would never marry anyone who wasn't interested in being buried alongside me, pure and simple!"

I wasn't sure what to say and asked, "Are you saying that because of this issue that surfaced, you don't think you want to see her again?"

"I really don't know," he responded. "I really liked her, but the cremation thing feels like a deal breaker for me."

I thought for a moment and then said, "Mark, if I were you, I'd worry more about living with a person at this point than dying with them." He couldn't help but laugh at the absurdity of the conversation. "Seriously," I continued, "I understand your concerns, but realize where we are in this process. There's a huge continuum between being on a first date and making final decisions with someone. A love relationship, which, of course, takes time, needs to be built before those issues can even be discussed. I've seen people make major changes for the right person, as they got to know them and became more committed to them. Suppose you fell in love and asked her to agree to a burial. Who's to say she wouldn't make that adjustment, given where you might be in your relationship? Of course, that's not something you could even know at this point, so it seems foolish to throw away any possibilities for an issue that's so far down the road. I recommend that you focus on the positives at this point and see if you can build on those."

Mark thought for a while and agreed to ask her out again. They had two more dates where neither of them mentioned the subject again, but the relationship never progressed any further. The deal breaker for Mark turned out to be Shelley's slow response time in returning his calls and her seeming need to control every aspect of their planning. While the outcome was disappointing, that concern, rather than some far-removed issue, made much more sense to me as a matchmaker trying to figure out where dating nonstarters occur.

Deal breakers come in all shapes and sizes. Sometimes the catalyst stems from a person's inability to see the other in the here and now and projecting their own interpretation of how they expect the other person to act in a given situation. Susan and Michael are perfect examples of this common first-date pitfall.

Susan was a very smart, attractive attorney in private practice in her midthirties. Michael was a law professor at a local law school in his late thirties. They were both interested in marriage and family. Their connection was instantaneous. Michael was drawn to her good looks, smarts, and values. Susan was physically attracted to Michael, liked his personality, and could see the potential between them.

After two dates, Michael called me to express his concerns. "I don't think she's 'the one,'" he stated.

"Why do you say that?" I asked.

"Well, don't get me wrong. She's fantastic. I totally understand why you matched us, but I don't think our goals are the same."

"How do you mean?" I asked.

"Well, she works so many hours," he said. "I can't see how that would work, if we had a family."

"Michael," I said, "I happen to know that Susan's primary goal is marriage and a family. Right now, she's a single woman working for a law firm. How else would she be spending her time?" I asked. "Also, she specifically told me during our initial consultation that if she were lucky enough to get married and have kids, she'd like to go part-time so that she could be a 'hands on' mom."

"Oh," he said. "I hadn't really thought about that. I suppose it's not fair to judge her based on her current situation."

"Exactly," I said, encouraged that he seemed to understand my point. "I also happen to know that she's very domestic, loves to entertain, and always volunteers to do the cooking for the law firm's annual picnic," I added.

That seemed to do the trick. He decided to keep seeing her and to remain open. I was delighted that I had gotten them over that "speed bump" at the outset of their relationship. Michael and Susan ended up dating exclusively for six months. Ironically, at that juncture, Susan decided to break up with him because, as she put it, she found him to be "too boring." How ironic that Michael was so quick to condemn her for her lifestyle, when ultimately, *he* turned out to be the reason for their breakup.

Another common mistake I have observed on first dates is people's tendency to share too much information about their divorces, breakups, or losses. While it's important for people to be honest about where they are in their emotional development when meeting someone for the first time, dwelling on the past, is never a good way to start an interaction. Some clients have reported extreme examples of this where they were tempted to hand their date an invoice for "therapeutic services rendered" at the end of their time together. No one wants to feel like a captive audience by someone who's venting about their past problems rather than trying to get to know them. This is a classic red flag, which should raise immediate concerns about getting involved with someone who has clearly not moved past a prior relationship.

> *While it's important for people to be honest about where they are in their emotional development when meeting someone for the first time, dwelling on the past, is never a good way to start an interaction.*

## CHAPTER NINETEEN

# Paradise Lost

*I*n the fall of 1995, my mother, who was terminally ill, began saying her goodbyes to her dearest friends. True to her character, one by one, she bravely called them and dealt with whatever unfinished business remained between them. Greta, one of her oldest friends and another Holocaust survivor from Germany, had a similar history. They had both left Germany as teenagers in time to save themselves and had lived in Israel for decades before moving to the United States. Greta had two children: Judy, a married daughter in Annapolis, and Yossi, a divorced son who lived in Hawaii and was fifteen years my senior. My mother and Greta decided to play matchmakers themselves and suggested that Yossi and I meet the next time he was in town to visit his sister.

I had heard about him throughout my childhood and had seen photos of him in my youth, but I had never met him due to the age difference between us. He was an avid traveler, loved to sail, and had spent much of his youth traveling the world. He had grown up in Israel and then in Yonkers, New York. In his early

twenties, he married Sherry, the daughter of another one of
their German friends. They later had a daughter, Daphna, from
whom he was now estranged. That marriage had lasted thirteen
years. Yossi had left Sherry very abruptly, causing her to have a
breakdown and an extended psychiatric hospitalization, which
Daphna never forgave him for. His second wife was a much
younger woman, who had been one of his graduate students. She
was Chinese and from Singapore. Their marriage lasted only three
years and did not produce any children, much to Greta's relief.

Yossi was now fifty and single again, living on a fifty-two-foot
sailboat in Honolulu. He traveled to the East Coast frequently to
develop a biotech company with some colleagues in New Jersey
and to visit family and friends. He was highly educated, with two
PhDs, one in public health, the other in geriatric medicine. He
was a short, muscular fellow with a beard and glasses. While not
particularly handsome, he seemed to exude a lot of charisma.

When Yossi called from Annapolis to make plans to get together,
I was apprehensive. After all, his track record wasn't all that great,
and I still mourned the loss of my relationship with Ian. I agreed
to go out with Yossi, despite my doubts. When we met at Houston's
in Rockville, Maryland, I could tell right away that he liked me. He
was cute, very smart, and had a great sense of humor. His life read
like an adventure novel. He confided that he missed being married
and shared that while he loved his lifestyle, he hoped to find a
partner to settle down with, whether that meant on land or sea.

I couldn't imagine being right for him, but his intense interest in
me was flattering nonetheless. He looked at me as if I were dessert,
and he made sure to order some so as to prolong our time together.
We spoke a lot about our families, which was very cathartic since
we'd both had similar upbringings due to our common legacy of
survival. At the end of the evening, he asked me whether he could
see me again while he was still in town. I agreed to have a second
date with him a few days later.

I conferred with my mother before our next date. She told me that she had spoken to Greta, who was delighted that Yossi liked me, and she was praying that something serious would come of it. My mother was completely onboard with the idea herself. I understood that one of her deepest regrets was that she would die before she could see me settled down once more. My divorce from Howard had taken a terrible toll on her, for which I felt tremendous guilt. The subsequent heartache that I carried from Ian was something that pained her deeply as well. Given her condition, I wanted to cheer her up, so I decided to see Yossi again and to keep an open mind about him. I wondered what I would do once she was gone and not around to advise me any longer.

Our second date was better than expected. I tried to avoid the inevitable comparisons to Ian. This was an entirely different circumstance and time. I told myself that I owed it to myself to give Yossi a chance.

Yossi worked so hard to entertain and charm me that I warmed to him even more over dinner. He filled in some more details about his life in Hawaii. Commuting back and forth from his boat by motorcycle, Yossi taught part-time at the University of Hawaii. I smiled at that mental image. I'd always liked men who drove motorcycles for some reason and felt encouraged by that. He told me about his group of friends, professionals who had come to Hawaii for a more laid-back lifestyle. They loved sailing and often served as his crew. They sounded like the kind of people I would like. He also told me about the company he was in the process of developing, which, as a businesswoman myself, intrigued me. I started to see possibilities with him. "Wouldn't my mother and Greta be happy?" I asked myself.

When we left the cozy Greek restaurant and stood alongside my car in the parking lot, he kissed me goodbye. It was nice, and while I didn't exactly feel any "bells and whistles," I told myself that I might be expecting too much too soon.

Yossi flew back to Hawaii the next day and made it a point of calling me every night from his boat. This required an adjustment, since I had gotten used to dealing with a five-hour time difference ahead with Ian in London. Hawaii is six hours behind, so I had to take a time difference into account once again. I mused about how nice it would be to have someone in my own time zone, but here I was, about to embark on another adventure with a man halfway around the world, only in the other direction.

Yossi's devotion to me was very endearing. He knew what my mother meant to me and was very sensitive to the pain I felt about losing her in the near future. It was very comforting for me to know that once she was gone, I'd have the connection to his family to support me.

The following month Yossi visited again for a week. This time, however, I invited him to stay with me. It felt like we were already in a relationship, and I was ready to welcome him into my home. Our first time together was bittersweet. I felt relieved that the room was dark so he couldn't see the tears I cried for Ian. I felt guilty about having those feelings for another man while I was with him but chose not to share them with Yossi. I didn't want him to feel like he was in another man's shadow and figured that I'd adjust over time. While I didn't feel a fraction of the passion for him that I had felt for Ian, it felt good to be with him, nonetheless. I told myself that Ian was history and that I simply had to move on.

The week we spent together turned out to be very enjoyable. It was nice to have his company. He accommodated my work schedule, wined and dined me, and even cooked for me a few times. We both loved Middle Eastern cuisine, given our backgrounds, and he made all my favorite dishes, which reminded me of my mother's cooking. By the end of that first week together, I began to warm to the idea of being Yossi's girlfriend.

When Yossi invited me to visit him, I eagerly agreed. My children were planning a trip with their father, so I had a week to myself and decided to fulfill my lifelong dream of visiting Hawaii. "What a great way to be introduced to Hawaii," I thought. I'd be hosted by him, have an adventure staying on his boat, and be shown around by a local. It sounded fabulous.

The flight over was interminable. There was a three-hour layover in Los Angeles, so the entire journey took about fifteen hours. By the time the plane landed, I was exhausted but exhilarated to be there. It was charming to receive leis as we exited the plane, which I'd seen in movies and on TV many times.

In the terminal, a local Polynesian band played as I followed signs to baggage claim. Yossi stood there in a multicolored Hawaiian shirt, shorts, and sandals with a huge smile. He was thrilled to see me, and we embraced warmly and then headed to the parking area to get his Jeep, which was his second vehicle.

Yossi and I chatted all the way to the harbor as I looked around, marveling at the tropical plants, flowers, and palm trees along the way. The air was crisp and, to my delight and surprise, not humid like I had expected. I had experienced tropical climates only in Florida and the Caribbean, where the humidity had been thick and oppressive. "No wonder they call this paradise," I thought, as I breathed in deeply. My hair would be frizz free!

We arrived at the marina where Yossi's boat was docked. I had already seen pictures of it but was even more impressed in person by how well cared for it was. The fifty-two-foot sailboat had wooden railings and floors, which gleamed in the sun. It was obvious how much pride Yossi took in maintaining it. He had warned me that it was small, so not to pack too much. This time, I listened and made sure to bring only the essentials with me.

We boarded his boat, which he named the *Shalom* in honor of his Israeli roots. The interior was compact but had everything he needed. It had a wonderfully cozy feel to it. His bedroom was located at the bow of the boat and had a double-sized bed with a porthole in the low ceiling from which one could see the stars at night. "How romantic," I thought.

Yossi made me feel very much at home on the *Shalom*. Other than the bathroom facilities, which I found somewhat challenging, it was great fun. He did not plan to take the boat out during my time there, since that would have involved crew and would have been a big production. He preferred to spend the time alone with me and show me around the island.

Before we set out to explore the following day, he received a fax (in the days before e-mail) from my mother that read, "I forbid you to take Leora out on your motorcycle!" We both had a tremendous laugh together over that. God bless her. Even in her weakened condition, she tried to look out for me. Soon, I'd have to start looking out for myself, but not yet. I called to tell her that I was safe and thanked her for her concern. I told her a white lie to reassure her, explaining that we'd be driving in his Jeep, so she had no reason to worry. I wasn't sure whether or not she was convinced, but she left it at that, either because she believed me or was too weak to argue.

It turned out to be a glorious week. I managed to put aside all of my troubles and enjoy being a tourist. The island itself was gorgeous and truly worthy of the name "paradise." I did some business while I was there as well.

I reached out to a local matchmaker named Shalaine who advertised in the local newspaper to inquire about whether she might have a match for a fifty-six-year-old gentleman named Philip, for whom I was recruiting potential prospects. She was delighted to hear from me and invited me to her office in downtown Honolulu. We had an instant rapport. She presented one of her most beautiful clients, Hillary, a forty-three-year-old former model, now real estate agent, as a potential match for Phillip. I phoned him from there, enthusiastically telling him all about her. He was interested, so we put them in touch, and during my week-long stay there, Philip and Hillary spoke on the phone three times and planned to figure out a way to meet each other. I was so excited to have made this unique match and felt like fate had brought me there for several reasons.

Over the next six months, Yossi and I continued to function as a couple. We spoke almost every night, and every month he'd spend a week with me working on his business while I worked on mine. We spent a great deal of time with his sister in Annapolis and her family, whom I enjoyed. She, along with their parents, continued to root for our deepening relationship.

At Yossi's urging, I arranged to travel back to Hawaii for a second visit. This time, Yossi planned an excursion around the Hawaiian Islands and arranged for four of his friends, whom I had met the last time I was there, to serve as crew. Yossi was a veteran sailor of over thirty years but cautioned me that the Hawaiian waters were notoriously rough, so the trip might be challenging. He insisted that I eat a hearty breakfast so that I wouldn't become nauseous. Our dream excursion, however, turned into a nightmare as I, along with Yossi (the captain) and the rest of the crew, became violently seasick. There was no relief in sight as the boat lurched mercilessly through the choppy waters. One by one, we all retched over the side of the boat, unable to even make it to "the head." By the time we reached our destination on the other side of the island, we all looked and felt like dishrags.

This was hardly the romantic experience I had had with him during my first visit; however, it gave me important data about Yossi and his friends. I discovered over the several days we spent together that they were dysfunctional in their professional, financial, and social lives. They had moved to Hawaii to find "paradise" but had, in reality, only brought their problems with them from the mainland. I wondered why Yossi was so tight with this group, whom I found difficult to relate to. Yossi's behavior on this excursion also concerned me. His arrogance at thinking that he was in perfect control of the situation quickly dissolved into defensiveness. Rather than handle the situation with humor, he blamed his crew members, who had only come to help, for the majority of the problems we encountered. That didn't sit well with me at all.

Once we were alone again, I couldn't shake the feeling that the infatuation stage in our relationship was over. I asked him about his long-term goals, and he didn't seem to have a solid plan, other than to continue teaching part-time at the university, which paid very little. It became obvious that he felt no pressure in that regard. He anticipated a large inheritance someday from his parents and therefore wasn't at all worried about establishing himself. It felt like I was dating Peter Pan. I shared my impression with him, which he was understandably insulted by. I also told him that if he was contemplating a future with me, it couldn't be on his boat exclusively. I had two children in school and wasn't going to move them to Hawaii away from their father and their lives in Bethesda. He suggested that we table the conversation for the time being and just get through the next few months of my mother's decline. I agreed.

I flew home eager to share the experience with my mother. I drove up to New York the following weekend with my children so that they could spend time with their grandmother, not knowing how long she had left. She rallied in our presence, and we had a wonderfully sweet visit together. She was pleased that things were going well with Yossi but, true to form, mirrored my concerns about him. She warned me that she wasn't sure whether he could actually make a good-enough living to be considered husband material. I told her that we were a long way away from that point, and, for now, I was happy. I didn't want to trouble her by sharing my own doubts, which had been gnawing at me since my return. She seemed to accept that and took comfort in knowing I wasn't alone.

When we said our goodbyes at the end of the weekend, it was heart-wrenching. My mother put up a brave front, but we both understood that the end was near. Immediately after we left, she declined and was taken to hospice. I got the call once I returned home, and I immediately turned back around and braved the New Jersey Turnpike back to New York to be at her side. I cried uncontrollably the entire time. As I went through a tollbooth along the way, the attendant waved me along and said that my fee had been paid by the fellow in the car ahead of me. I was taken aback. He said that the fellow had given him a message for me that "A pretty girl like me shouldn't be so sad." I thought that that was one of the kindest gestures I'd ever received, which made me cry even harder.

My mother was in hospice for three days, where my sister and I took turns sitting vigil at her bedside. The night before she died, a friend called and asked if she could take me out to dinner near the hospital, figuring that I hadn't eaten much all day. I said that they had just given my mom a shot of morphine, so I knew that she'd be out for a while and I could therefore break away for a bit. Then she asked where I wanted to go. I listed a few options that I knew of in the neighborhood.

Shockingly, my mother opened her eyes and exclaimed, "Oh the Del Rio Diner. That's a good one. Go there!" Then she closed her eyes and fell back into the drug-induced sleep from which she had awakened.

My friend heard the conversation over the phone. "Was that your mother?" she asked.

"Yes," I replied. "Ever the Jewish mother."

How amazing that even in her morphine-induced stupor, she was still giving me advice. It was actually the last piece of advice she ever gave me. She finally succumbed when neither my sister nor I were present for a brief time. Thankfully, I got back just in time to hold her hand and tell her that I loved her as she took her last breath.

While I had braced myself for the inevitable, when my mother finally died, I was completely bereft. I was actually relieved that Yossi wasn't with me through the funeral and subsequent shiva, or mourning period, so that I didn't have to worry about him and could be fully present with my family and friends who were there to support me in my grief. I probably should have paid closer attention to those feelings of relief but was overwhelmed with so much emotion at that time that my relationship with Yossi was the last thing on my mind.

After I returned from New York, where the funeral had taken place, I tried to pick up the pieces and function normally, but it was a major struggle. The nightly calls from Yossi helped tremendously. I could tell he was falling deeper and deeper for me. While I knew didn't feel quite the same way about him, I still enjoyed the attention and the benefits of being in a relationship, given my emotional fragility.

Come December, Yossi planned a trip to New York for his birthday and asked me to join him. He would fly into DC, and we would drive up together. He said he'd been lying awake on his boat night after night pondering how we could make a life together, and he had a plan he wanted to discuss with me during that drive. I was intrigued.

Yossi flew in on a Thursday evening, and the following morning, we drove north. Somewhere between Baltimore and Delaware, he shared his plan with me. He said that he wanted us to marry and, while this wasn't an actual proposal, he wanted to share his vision of how this would all work. He had had a dream of sailing his boat from Hawaii to Israel and settling back in Israel where he believed he had a multitude of job prospects. He suggested that I, along with my daughter, Elana, join him in Israel, leaving my son, Adam, with his father during the school year. During the summer, he continued, I'd switch children, and have Adam spend his summers in Israel.

I was dumbstruck. "That's your plan?" I said. "In all this time we've been together, did you really think I'd go for that? Do you really think I'd leave my autistic son behind and only see him two months a year? Do you even know me at all? Also, have you not been listening? You know I'm going through a bitter custody battle with my ex, so how on earth could I even think of taking Elana out of the country?" I was floored.

"Please, don't be upset," he pleaded. "This is only a first draft. Everything is negotiable."

I sat in silence trying to process what had just happened. His "big plan" had gone over like a lead balloon. His lack of understanding and sensitivity to my situation astonished me. This was the last thing I had expected. I actually thought he might propose that he move to DC and get a job in his field or continue building his company while I raised my children. We could sail on his boat during school breaks and summers but would have a primary home in my area. Instead, he wanted me to separate my children and essentially abandon my developmentally challenged son. That was his brilliant plan. "No wonder he's estranged from his own daughter and not plagued with guilt," I thought. It was all about *him*. I was heartsick and realized at that moment that he was not the man I could build a future with.

The rest of Yossi's visit went by in a blur. We stayed with his parents, who were still praying that an engagement was in the offing. His mother even told me that they would happily pay for the entire wedding. I tried my best not to show how distressed I really was and somehow got through the visit. "No sense in bursting their bubble while I'm here," I thought. Afterward, Yossi planned to fly back to Hawaii from New York, and I was to drive back to DC by myself. Our parting was sad and awkward. He had gotten my message of disappointment loud and clear and had no

clue how to rehabilitate himself in my eyes. While I felt sorry for
him, I couldn't pretend that things would be okay. I kissed him
tearfully and thanked him for everything he had done for me. I
didn't actually say goodbye, but I might as well have.

When I finally adjusted to functioning on my own, in my own
time zone, I had time to reflect on my long-distance experiences,
which were completely different
from one another. Conventional
wisdom would say that people
who engage in serial long-distance
relationships have commitment
challenges and therefore choose
someone far away. I didn't think
that applied in my case, since
I had been married and was
still going through the divorce
process. The long-distance option made perfect sense during this
transition in my life.

> **Conventional wisdom
> would say that people who
> engage in serial long-
> distance relationships have
> commitment challenges
> and therefore choose
> someone far away.**

My relationship with Ian was unlike any other I'd had.
The strength of my connection to him on all levels, physical,
intellectual, emotional, and spiritual, was extraordinary. I felt so
blessed, despite its loss, to have had that kind of love in my life,
something many people never even come close to experiencing.
Perhaps, as my mother had suggested, it was so extraordinary
*precisely* because it was temporary. Trying to turn something so
magical and ephemeral into a permanent day-to-day relationship
would have changed its nature fundamentally. I took comfort in
knowing that his new wife, while being the one who "won" him
permanently, would never experience that same level of magic
with him as I'd had. It would have to be different, by definition.
I cherished the memories of its uniqueness and knew that he too
would carry those memories forever. In fact, during our parting
conversation, he told me that I was a "legend" in South London,
the one from across the pond who had captured and opened his

heart. I liked being a legend. It helped me cope with the grief of losing him. I also understood that he had set the bar higher than it had ever been set before, in terms of the right relationship. After Ian, I couldn't settle.

Yossi would have been settling. His arrival on the scene during one of the worst chapters in my life was a true blessing, but it wasn't love, at least not on my part. It was an exciting distraction from my problems and, admittedly, a crutch to support me through the death of my beloved mother. How wonderful for me that they had known each other and he could therefore understand what that loss had meant to me. His friendship was a gift in my life at that time but simply not meant to be forever. How fortunate for me that I now understood the difference.

## CHAPTER TWENTY

# It Takes Two

In her midforties, Brenda was the CFO of an international accounting firm whose headquarters was based in London. She'd never been married and had no children. Although she lived and owned a home in Washington, DC, after having several relationships with local men, she decided to hire me to help her find a permanent relationship. When we met for the first time, she shared her frustration about still being single. After all, she felt that she was reasonably attractive, which I found to be quite an understatement. She was gorgeous, successful, and "had her head on her shoulders," as she put it. She couldn't understand why the right man hadn't come along so far and was therefore willing to go to great lengths to meet someone special.

Coincidentally, I was planning a trip to London within a month of our consultation and suggested that she might consider having me recruit a British man for her while I was there.

Her eyes lit up, and she jumped at the idea. "I've always found English men to be so charming," she said. "I'm not sure why this hadn't occurred to me before. My company is based there, and my married brother, whom I adore, lives in Kensington, in South London. I could definitely see myself living over there," she exclaimed. "Why not?"

"Well, whatever your reasons for not pursuing this in the past," I ventured, "there's no time like the present."

I proposed a plan, which consisted of tapping into my local contacts, responding to personal ads (in the pre-Internet dating era), and possibly placing ads of our own in local publications. Once there, I purchased a *Time Out London* magazine, which listed everything that was happening in town and had an extensive "Personals" section for people looking to meet. I perused columns of ads and then came upon a promising one from a man named Oliver, an accountant in his own practice living in North London.

I called the number in the ad and was pleased to get Oliver on the phone right away. I explained the purpose of my call and that I represented Brenda, who was looking to meet a special man about his age. We ended up having a wonderful conversation about him, his family, interests, etc. After providing him with a detailed description of Brenda, he expressed an interest in meeting her and invited me to join him in his private gentleman's club for tea so that I could show him Brenda's photo and learn more about him in order to be able to make a sound recommendation to Brenda.

I walked into an impressive private club, where I immediately became aware of the fact that I was the only female in the room. Women could come as guests but were not admitted as members into the club. I wasn't concerned with all of that. My agenda was clear, and I was impressed that Oliver took the time to meet with me in such auspicious surroundings. After our lengthy phone conversation, we had developed an instant rapport, and we continued where we left off. I found him to be an enchanting fellow: intelligent, personable, and undeniably handsome. He was tall with blond hair, green eyes, and a short, cropped beard. Had

I been looking myself, he would have been someone I would have happily dated, which was a standard I often used for screening prospects for clients about my age. While I could tell he was very open to the idea of meeting Brenda, when I showed him her photo, he was sold.

After spending almost two hours together, we came to the mutual conclusion that meeting Brenda made sense, presuming she would approve of his photo once I returned home and could report to Brenda regarding my meeting with Oliver. I let him know that, presuming she was interested, she had a business trip to London in the near future and could possibly meet in the next month or so. After I left, I excitedly called Brenda to tell her about Oliver and to let her know that I enthusiastically recommended "the match."

Brenda was impressed that I had come up with such a desirable prospect and said that based on my description, and the fact that she trusted my judgment, she couldn't think of a reason why it wouldn't make sense for her to meet him.

A month later, Brenda and Oliver met for dinner at a trendy restaurant in London's West End. They clicked immediately and had a fantastic first date, which delighted her. She wisely made sure to arrange her schedule so that she could see him every day she was there for the next four days. By the time she flew home, they both felt like they had found something special in each other.

Their romance continued over the next six months, mostly with Brenda traveling to London for work. Wanting to visit her in her environment, Oliver also made two trips over to see her. He looked forward to enjoying the sights of Washington, DC, with Brenda as his guide. Brenda reported that she was happier than she'd been in a very long time. As such, I had high hopes that their relationship would blossom into a deeper level of commitment.

That summer, however, Brenda called to tell me that she had decided not to continue seeing Oliver. I was crestfallen. "What happened?" I inquired.

"Nothing happened," she answered. "I like him a lot but have decided that I really don't want to live in London after all."

I was stunned to hear this. After all, the plan from the start was that if she met someone special in London, she would move there, given her connections to that city. Apparently, in the six months they were together, Oliver had not won her heart sufficiently to have her entertain the idea of a permanent move. Meanwhile, I had heard from Oliver every few months, and he had expressed his eternal gratitude for my having introduced him to Brenda. He was clearly besotted with her, and my heart ached for him, knowing how devastated he'd be about the relationship ending.

I tried to understand why Oliver hadn't been able to capture Brenda's heart, but in the end, it simply boiled down to the fact that while she enjoyed her time with him, she never actually fell in love with him. I realized that regardless of how desirable a match I thought they were, love had to exist between them, and if there was an imbalance in their feelings for each other, the relationship would eventually fail.

> **Regardless of how desirable a match I thought they were, love had to exist between them, and if there was an imbalance in their feelings for each other, the relationship would eventually fail.**

No amount of wishful thinking on their matchmaker's part could supply that magic ingredient.

Disappointed as I was for them, I accepted the reality that pulling up stakes and starting a new life overseas simply wasn't in the cards for Brenda. She thanked me profusely, letting me know what a great job I had done in finding Oliver for her and that she would always cherish their time together, but we needed to keep looking.

Rather than dragging the process out for years only to come to the same conclusion, at least she had reached her decision fairly quickly. While Oliver would be unhappy in the short run, he wouldn't have invested years with someone who wasn't willing to commit to a life with him. Brenda was also better off reaching her conclusion sooner rather than later, so that, with my support, she could focus on a more permanent prospect.

## CHAPTER TWENTY-ONE

# A Cautionary Tale

The winter of 1995 was grim. I was grieving the loss of my mother, still in the throes of a bitter custody battle and divorce from Howard, experiencing significant financial challenges, and newly single. Now that both my long-distance relationships were a thing of the past, I no longer felt cushioned by the security they had provided. This made a huge difference in my emotional equilibrium. I felt completely alone for the first time. While I had been the one to end the last relationship, finding myself without one was a shock to my system. Despite these challenges, I tried to be the best mother I knew how, to two children with very different but significant needs.

Elana, then age ten, had been very close to my mother and grieved her loss as well. In addition, she had to cope with splitting her time between her father's place and mine while dealing with an undercurrent of hostility between her parents. I tried my best to surround her with loving family and friends during this difficult time. I brought my father down from New York for an extended visit so that we could support each other in our grief.

Adam, age seven, withdrew further into himself, seemingly because of his autism. He did not express any grief directly. It took much greater effort to engage him, effort I found myself hard pressed to muster. While I managed to get him to all of his therapy appointments, play groups, and social activities, I felt emotionally vacant as I went about meeting those responsibilities.

My business was my major coping mechanism. Finding happiness for my clients provided an uplifting balance to my own circumstances and fulfilled me at a time when there was little else to feel happy about. All I could do was put one foot in front of the other as I continued to build my business. I took comfort in knowing that my mother would have wanted me to forge ahead accordingly.

During the holiday season, I was invited to attend a networking event at the River Club, a very popular, upscale jazz club in Georgetown. It was one of the only venues in DC that offered quality live music and dancing in an appealing environment for singles and couples alike. This particular event was geared toward singles and offered an opportunity to mingle with a high-end crowd and prospect for new business, as well as potential matches for my clients. This was the first time I attended a social event since my mother's death.

In the Orthodox Jewish tradition, mourners do not attend parties for an entire year after the loss of a parent. While I wasn't religious myself, I still felt guilty about attending a party so soon after my mother's death. I rationalized that it was a work function, rather than a party, and something my mother would have encouraged. In her honor, I wore a black velvet dress, which I had found among her collection of evening dresses. It fit me loosely. I was much taller and slimmer than she, and the hemline fell at tea rather than ankle length on me. It looked great, and it comforted me to wear something of hers that was both elegant and fitting for the occasion.

I arrived at the club as the live music was about to start. As I sipped on a glass of Chardonnay, I began to feel less tense about being there. I ran into several people whom I knew, as was often the case at singles' events, and spent the early part of the evening chatting with them and being introduced to their friends as well. They asked for my card, which I happily distributed. "This is my purpose in being here after all," I reassured myself. I worked the crowd for a few hours until my feet began to ache from my high heels. I took a seat on one of the upholstered couches in the main area.

A tall, very handsome gentleman approached and asked me to dance. I politely declined, explaining that I was there to work that evening. He was intrigued by that and asked me what I did. Realizing he might have gotten the wrong idea, I ventured further. "I'm a matchmaker," I said. He seemed to get a kick out of that and introduced himself as Wayne. Without asking, Wayne took a seat next to me. I introduced myself and told him about my business. He then asked for my card, examined it, and made it clear that he was not interested in my services but, rather, in me. I was flattered.

As we talked further, I learned that he was Jewish, in business himself, and divorced with two children. He bought me another drink. I told him that I had recently lost my mother and wasn't there to party and again emphasized that I was there strictly to promote my business. I shared how close my mother and I had been and how devastating her loss was to me. He then looked me in the eye and said, "She sent me." Tears welled up in my eyes as I fantasized that to be true.

The rest of the evening passed in a blur. I continued to flirt with Wayne and enjoyed the music. As midnight approached, I suddenly felt exhausted and told him that it was time for me to leave. He graciously took my valet ticket, which he paid, and arranged for the valet to retrieve my car as I left the club. I thanked him, told him it was nice to have met him, and wished him happy holidays, sensing I'd be hearing from him again.

As I drove home, I pondered Wayne's statement about my mother. "Slick move on his part," I told myself. Yet, part of me wanted to believe that meeting him was a heaven-sent gift from my mom, who was still looking out for me and didn't want me to be alone.

I hadn't been home fifteen minutes when my phone rang. It was about 1:00 a.m. "Who could be calling me at this hour?" I thought apprehensively. I picked up my landline, which also served as my business phone, and to my surprise, it was Wayne.

"Sorry to be calling so late. I wanted to make sure you got home okay," he said.

I was impressed. "Thanks," I said. "I appreciate that."

"One other thing," he said. "I just wanted to tell you that you're going to be my next girlfriend."

I had no idea how to respond. Part of me was delighted that I had made such an impression on him. The other, more rational part of me, was skeptical, but I simply laughed and said, "Really? Oh, okay, goodnight," and hung up.

That was the beginning of an elaborate trap, which I had no idea Wayne had set for me but which I predictably fell into. He mounted a major romantic onslaught, which was impossible to resist. For our first date, he picked La Ferme, a pricey and romantic French restaurant in Chevy Chase, Maryland. He also insisted that he pay for my babysitter, something no one else had ever offered.

Once we got to the restaurant, Wayne listened sympathetically to my problems with my children and shared his own experience of having raised two of his own, one of whom was battling drug addiction. He had been married a second time and had been a stepfather to two other children during their formative years, something he was quite proud of. He spoke about the issues in both his marriages and painted a picture of a man who, despite his best intentions, was the victim of difficult circumstances in both relationships. He shared that he loved children and that he was open to a new family at some point.

Adam's autism didn't seem to daunt him. He claimed to want to find meaning in his life by being part of a child's life with challenges. This played perfectly into all the needs and insecurities that a mom in my situation would have. He was in insurance sales, having built up a clientele, according to him, from working in his first wife's family business. I presumed he was doing well, based on the extravagant dinner he treated me to and the generosity he demonstrated.

For our second date, Wayne offered to come over and bring dinner on a night when my kids were with their father. I wasn't sure whether or not it was too soon to have an in-home date, but he convinced me that it would be much cozier than going out on that winter night. I was very attracted to him and worried that I might be tempted to sleep with him that night, but I reluctantly agreed.

Wayne showed up with flowers, lobster, and champagne, ready to woo me passionately. It worked like a charm. I found myself putty in his hands as he skillfully seduced me. He seemed to have an inside track into my desires and made sure to please me, rather than focusing on himself, something I found noteworthy. I was impressed. Within a matter of weeks, I became his new girlfriend, something he had predicted from day one.

It was a whirlwind romance. He skillfully courted me and became the lover he instinctively knew I desired. For my part, I was just happy to feel good again. His lovemaking seemed to be the antidote to my grief, and it numbed me from the acute pain I had been feeling before we met.

But slowly, Wayne began to reveal that his business and family life were not the rosy picture he had painted for me at first. I learned that his company was on the verge of bankruptcy and his children were essentially estranged from him, except for frequent requests for money from his son, who was a heroin addict. By then, I was already "hooked" and making excuses in my own mind for his problems in order to justify remaining in the relationship with him.

After a few months together, I felt the time was right to introduce him to my children. Wayne's need to spend time with me began to spill over into time I had with my kids. They had not been exposed to my other boyfriends, but since Wayne had expressed a desire to build a serious relationship with me, I felt comfortable taking that next step.

Wayne was amazing with my children at first. He was kind and nurturing toward my son, as well as charismatic and charming with my daughter. He seduced them as skillfully as he had courted me, bringing them gifts and planning fun outings together. They were loving children and bonded with him fairly quickly. They were also happy to see me emerge from my depression. He brought an exciting, upbeat energy into our family dynamic, something that had been sorely lacking before his arrival on the scene.

That Valentine's Day, Wayne invited all of us to dinner at Hamburger Hamlet, one of my kids' favorite restaurants at that time. He had carefully chosen cute little gifts for them, which surprised and delighted them. I had gotten him an elegant cashmere scarf, which I gave him at dinner. He then presented me with a small suede jewelry box. I wondered what he had up his sleeve, since I understood that it was way too soon to even be thinking about an engagement. I opened the box. Inside was a one-carat diamond solitaire on a yellow gold chain. I gasped at such an unexpected and extravagant gift. I wasn't sure whether to be impressed or wary of this dramatic gesture. I chose to see it as a positive symbol that he was "all in" regarding our relationship and snuffed out those nagging doubts that were beginning to plague me.

The next step in Wayne's plan was to get me onboard with the idea of having him move in with me. It was now clear to me that his business was going under, but he reassured me that once he filed for bankruptcy, he would reincorporate and simply start another company with his existing clientele, who he claimed were loyal to him. He professed his love for me, said he wanted to be with me all the time, and promised to contribute financially to my household, if we lived together. This would still be cheaper than his paying his own rent and would assist me as well.

The idea was tempting, but I told him that for my children's sake, I didn't want to bring a man into my home unless we were heading toward marriage. I was concerned about the message I would be sending them. I wanted them to understand that marriage, not cohabitation, was my goal and living with a man on a casual basis was not consistent with my values. Wayne understood and promised that within six months, if everything went well, he would be prepared to get engaged. That reassured me, since I still felt guilty about everything my kids had been through from my divorce from their father, which had taken a total of three years to finalize. Bringing a loving stepfather into their lives, I reasoned, would be therapeutic for them and give me the stability I needed as well.

Living with Wayne started out like a dream come true. He was a passionate and attentive lover, a nurturing friend to my children when they were with us, and a financial support to me at a time when I really needed it. He offered to drive my daughter's carpool to school at 6:30 a.m. in the freezing cold, knowing what a struggle the early mornings were for me. He also waited with my son for the school bus on those frigid winter mornings. We began to feel like a family. We often interacted with his family, who were delighted to see him with someone as special as they considered me to be.

True to his word, that spring, Wayne proposed to me with a gorgeous diamond ring his jeweler friend had sold him, which he had gotten as the result of someone else's misfortune. I tried not to be superstitious about that and eagerly accepted his proposal. The kids were thrilled. This was exactly what I had wanted all along.

I had seen Wayne through his bankruptcy and supported him in establishing his new insurance company, for which he rented commercial space in Bethesda. My business was doing well at that time, and I loaned him money to get him started. We planned a small wedding in Disney World in Orlando so that we could give my kids the Disney vacation I had always wanted them to have.

Meanwhile, my family did their best to express their happiness for me, but I could tell that they didn't like him. My sister, Evie, the psychologist, told me that she had never had a more negative visceral reaction toward anyone in her life. My father, who was elderly and in poor health at that time, was just happy that I had someone to "take care of me." My friends were happy for me, but I could sense that they were polite around Wayne, rather than being genuinely fond of him. I tried not to let it bother me, but I couldn't help but be disappointed that they didn't embrace him as warmly as I had hoped.

My dream fiancé began to show signs that the "best behavior" routine he had presented to me in the beginning was eroding and his flawed, true self was emerging. He had bouts of depression when he became sullen and noncommunicative with me. When I tried to help, he would become angry and critical. I did my best to be a kind and nurturing partner, but I began to feel my self-esteem declining with each upsetting new incident between us. I shielded my children from these episodes as best as I could; they were still happy and excited that we were getting married.

As Wayne and I planned the details of our wedding trip, it became fodder for arguments rather than the happy experience I had envisioned. Despite my concerns, I forged ahead, determined to make this new marriage a success. We found a local rabbi, whom we hired to officiate, and arranged for flowers, a photographer, a harpist, and an intimate, yet lavish wedding dinner on the Disney property for our small party of twelve. The wedding party included my sister and her children, Wayne's brother and family, and my first cousin Harriet. To my bitter disappointment, my father was too ill at that time to travel to Orlando.

We had planned to have our ceremony in a scenic outdoor spot on a lake, with a quaint bridge, surrounded by tropical flowers and trees. Instead, when we got to Orlando, the temperature suddenly dropped into the forties, so we had to hold it inside, in a hotel meeting room that could have existed anywhere. I tried not to let all these disappointments affect me, but I couldn't help feeling like the signs were against us. Nevertheless, we had a lovely ceremony and then retired to the restaurant for our wedding dinner.

The restaurant was a five-star establishment, which we were excited to try for our special occasion. Oddly, when we sat down, we were not served by anyone for quite some time. I got up to see to the problem, and, to my amazement, Wayne followed me out into the hallway and screamed at me, calling me a "demanding bitch" and instructed me to sit back down and wait. I was stunned that he had spoken to me in that manner at our wedding dinner but didn't want to make a scene, so I complied.

The rest of the meal passed in a blur. When dessert was over, Wayne stood up and handed me an ornately wrapped box containing a wedding gift, which he encouraged me to open at the table. It was an ankle bracelet, something I had never worn before, with yellow gold and diamond block letters separated by a yellow gold chain and tiny pearls that spelled out the words *Just Married*. Everyone exclaimed what an unusual gift it was. I could hear my sister mutter that I had just been given a glorified "ball and chain."

The rest of our wedding weekend was miserable. Wayne behaved terribly to both me and the kids as I tried to show them a good time at the resort. It was as if a switch had suddenly flipped and my dream wedding trip had turned into a nightmare. I felt like I had just entered the twilight zone and was having trouble assimilating the experience. He pressured me not to see the rest of the family who were in town for the wedding. I felt terrible but didn't want them seeing him like that, so I shamefully caved to his demands. We somehow got through the weekend and flew home on Sunday night.

On Monday morning, I phoned the rabbi who had married us. I sheepishly asked him if he had sent in the paperwork yet, hoping that he had delayed submitting the forms to the clerk's office and could simply tear them up. I told him how embarrassed I was to be asking this but that I felt I had made a terrible mistake. He was taken aback and said that he had never been asked that question before in his entire career.

"I'm so sorry," he told me. "I already sent it in, so you'll need to consult a divorce attorney at this point." I was humiliated and crushed to hear this but still determined to make the best out of a bad situation. I told Wayne that I refused to be held hostage in any marriage after what my kids and I had already been through and the only way I would stay married to him was if we went into couples therapy to address what had just occurred. He, too, was embarrassed to be having that conversation on the heels of our wedding, and he agreed to go into therapy with me.

We saw a very skilled and experienced couples therapist named Nancy once a week for almost a year. Her intake process involved meeting as a couple and having individual sessions with each of us so that she could arrive at an assessment of the marriage. During subsequent sessions, Wayne would acknowledge the behaviors that had led us into therapy and promised to improve. He said everything he thought Nancy needed to hear in order for her to encourage us to continue to work on our marriage.

## CHAPTER TWENTY-TWO

# Divine Justice

*I* had high hopes for a recent couple who met through my practice in the fall and had been dating exclusively for two months. I considered that a major accomplishment since Seth, my sixty-five-year-old client, had been a challenge. Although he'd been in many long-term relationships in his life, he'd never been married, nor had any children. He was an established psychiatrist in his own practice and an intense and serious man who claimed to have a great sense of humor, although I never experienced that side of him in our work together.

Physically, he was reasonably handsome, tall, and fit, but his standards were much higher when it came to a woman's looks. He found himself attracted only to extremely pretty women who didn't always feel the same attraction toward him. When he first consulted me, he explained that the primary barrier in his past relationships had been a lack of chemistry on his part, even with a woman whom he'd been with for over two years. This confused me. I queried him further. What had their sex life actually been like for him to assert a blanket lack of chemistry between them?

He explained that they had had regular sex but that it had become "routine," and he no longer found it as exciting as it had been at first. I assumed he must have been aroused enough to consummate their lovemaking every time, so he couldn't have completely lost interest. I wondered what it would take to have him fully engaged in a fulfilling, romantic, and sexual relationship.

I worked tirelessly for Seth, introducing him to nine women in the first ten months of our contract. Only two of the women were up to his standards. The first was Diane, who was a dead ringer for the actress Sharon Stone. She was a gorgeous, classy fifty-eight-year-old blonde, who was ambivalent about him on their first date. In his enthusiasm to see her a second time, he unwittingly turned her off with his intensity. He told her that he found her to be attractive "from the minute he laid eyes on her" and "couldn't stop thinking about her ever since." This might not have been fatal had she been more interested in him, but because she sensed an air of desperation in his efforts to see her again, she decided that she was no longer interested.

Barbara, a petite woman with curly brown hair and a perfect figure, liked him until he tried to take her hand as they were crossing the street on their way to the garage after their dinner date. As she explained it to me, she felt as if he wasn't honoring her personal space when he took her hand without any signals on her part that she would welcome physical contact. Although I tried to persuade Barbara to give him another chance and to communicate her needs more clearly, she declined to reconsider. After both experiences, I coached Seth to pay more careful attention to the signals his date was communicating so that he could more effectively gauge her level of interest before professing his feelings for her or attempting to make physical contact. The seven other women whom I introduced him to didn't appeal to him, despite the fact that a few of them had liked him and would have wanted to see him again.

I was delighted when Seth seemed to hit it off with Theresa, my most recent referral. I took pride in the coaching that I gave him so he would present himself in the best possible light. Theresa was a beautiful, sweet sixty-year-old occupational therapist who was divorced with a grown son who lived in California. She was somewhat fragile, as she still mourned the loss of her twin sister a year earlier. My instincts told me that Seth, with his clinical skills, could be a comforting presence in her life.

After their first date, she reported that she was attracted to him, both physically and intellectually, and liked his personality. I was encouraged by this feedback since Seth was apparently working hard to tone down his intensity and take it one step at a time. A month later, Seth e-mailed me with an update, letting me know that they were dating exclusively. This was a significant achievement for him. I responded with my best wishes that something special would blossom between them.

Unfortunately, a month later, Seth wrote to inform me that Theresa had just e-mailed him to tell him that she was no longer interested in seeing him. He had asked her for a reason, but she demurred, stating that she just didn't think they were the "right match." Seth was disappointed and upset. I told him that I would be speaking with Theresa myself and if there were any insights that I could offer him, I certainly would.

Shortly thereafter, Theresa called to report that she had ended things with Seth. She confided in me that she had discovered that once they became intimate, he was awkward and clumsy, starting with the way he kissed her. "What a shame," I thought. Here Seth had been complaining about the lack of chemistry on his part toward most women, when, apparently, *he* didn't have the basic skills himself to keep the passion alive between him and Theresa.

If that were their only problem, this might have been overcome with time, open communication, and possibly sex therapy. His temperament, however, began to concern her over time as well.

She said that while she enjoyed his intelligence, his energy was extremely serious and intense. She had tried to "lighten things up" between them, but he was unable to shed the heaviness, which she began to experience as oppressive. That, along with the physical issues between them, led her to conclude that it was time to move on.

I comprehended what she was saying and didn't try to persuade her to give it more time, which I might have had I truly thought there was potential between them. She was convinced of her position, and it was my job to express empathy for her and to support her in her decision. I assured her that if Seth asked me what she had reported to me, I would be sure to protect her confidentiality; I would tell him that while she had enjoyed their time together, she didn't think the chemistry was there for *her*.

"Divine justice for Seth on some level," I mused. I still wanted to help him, though, and let him know that he had done well, but it apparently was just not "meant to be." I told him that dating required a bit of a thick skin to tolerate the ups and downs but at least he had been "back in the game" and was better equipped to navigate any future relationships as a result of his experience with Theresa. That seemed to resonate with Seth and helped soften the blow of Theresa's rejection.

## CHAPTER TWENTY-THREE

# A Final Decision

*I*n the midst of my struggle to keep my marriage to Wayne intact, my father, who had moved to Fort Lauderdale a year after my mother's death, took a turn for the worse. Since he had moved to Florida, he had been in and out of hospitals due to congestive heart failure, and his death was imminent. He had been a dialysis patient for almost twenty years, and his system was beginning to shut down.

Evie and I took turns visiting our father in Florida. It was my turn to fly down. I hurriedly packed the necessities I needed, including a dress suitable for a funeral.

Wayne drove me to the airport in my car and noticed that the gas tank was on empty. He began berating me for neglecting to fill the car with gas. I tearfully responded that I didn't need him to give me a hard time about something so petty, given what I was going through with my dad. My pleas fell on deaf ears, and he continued his tirade as we approached the airport. I was so upset by then that I told him to stop so I could get out of the car before we even got to the terminal. I opened the car door, but he continued to drive. I was nearly dragged along the pavement. A nearby police officer observed this and drove over to ask if all was well. Wayne, in his usual style, pretended that everything was fine and told the officer that his assistance wasn't needed. I was in such a state that I just nodded and got back into the car long enough to let Wayne drop me at the terminal. Had my father not been dying, I would have left Wayne then and there; however, I couldn't focus on that at the time. I needed to muster all my emotional reserves to handle the situation with my dad that was waiting for me in Florida.

I went straight from the airport to the hospital and was greeted by Hannah, my stepmother, the woman my father had married only seven months earlier. Hannah and my father had known each other as children in Poland. Her older sister had been married to my father's older brother, so they were part of each other's extended family. That couple, along with both sets of parents and four siblings, had perished in the Holocaust.

Hannah had had a mad crush on my father as a teenager because of his good looks and outgoing personality. In fact, she carried an old photo of him at age fifteen in her wallet for decades. She had gone on to marry and divorce twice and had recently been discharged from a psychiatric hospital before reconnecting with my father, who had had his own matchmaker.

Hannah's brother, Hershel, had been a client of my mother's travel agency for decades and knew of her illness. After she passed away, he contacted my father to suggest that my father reach out to Hannah, who was now divorced, living in Florida, and would love to hear from him. My father called her, and, as Hershel had predicted, she was thrilled to hear from him. She immediately invited him to fly down and visit her.

After that visit, my father returned to New York and announced to my sister and me that he would be moving in with her in Florida and that they would be married.

"Daddy," I said to him at the time, "are you sure you know what you're doing? What do you know about Hannah?" I asked. "After all, she clearly has some serious mental health problems, having just been in a psych hospital."

"Leora'le," he responded, "I'm a sick man and need someone to take care of me, but I still have all my marbles. She's a strong woman and wants to do the job. So what if she's a little *meshuggah* (Yiddish for "crazy")? I'll do the thinking for the two of us. It's a good match!"

My father had always loved Florida and considered it paradise. What could I say? He was almost eighty years old, alone, and did not want to be a burden to my sister or me; he was determined to give it a try. Hannah, in turn, chomped at the bit to fulfill her childhood fantasy of marrying my father. At almost eighty, he was still quite a handsome man, and she would now have a partner to live out their lives together.

My sister and I threw a small wedding, officiated by a rabbi, for the family in a restaurant in Manhattan. The rabbi only performed the religious ceremony in order to make my father, who was very traditional, comfortable. He never certified it as a civil marriage so that my sister's and my financial interests would be protected. My father had worked out a very generous agreement with Hannah, who was estranged from her own children and financially challenged. He would pay her a certain amount of money for each year he lived with her. She agreed, eager to accept him on any terms. During the wedding party, my father wryly told me, "I'm on the right track, as long as I don't derail."

A distraught Hannah, who had been sitting vigil at my father's bedside, bringing him food, which he could barely touch, greeted me at the hospital. My sister had speculated that my father had deteriorated so rapidly since moving down to Florida because Hannah had encouraged him to stray from his dialysis diet, thus causing his system to begin breaking down. That made sense.

My mother had been a stickler for making sure that she cooked him foods low in potassium, which enabled him to survive on dialysis for almost twenty years. To live on dialysis that long was highly unusual. Hannah didn't have the patience or the skills to continue the same regimen and began pressuring him to go out often and eat at her favorite Chinese restaurant, which was toxic to his system. He fell deathly ill within seven months of his move to Florida. His doctor informed me that there was nothing he could do for him except make him comfortable, so Hannah and I began the waiting game together. As I witnessed her anguish, I realized how much she loved him and tried to think of her as his "angel of mercy" rather than the crazy woman who had caused his demise. At least he would leave this earth being dearly loved, something that gave me comfort in my grief.

My father died two days later. My brother-in-law, Joe, arranged to have his body flown to New York for the funeral. He was to be laid to rest next to my mother in their cemetery plot on Long Island.

I was still fuming from the incident at the airport with Wayne yet had no choice but to put my anger aside and ask him to drive my kids from Bethesda to New York for their grandfather's service, while I flew directly from Fort Lauderdale into JFK airport. Wayne stepped up appropriately and publicly played the part of the supportive husband and stepfather over the next few days. In private, however, he was cold and punishing toward me.

My kids had to return to school, and Wayne was unwilling to continue to care for them on his own. He insisted that I drive home with him and the kids, rather than remain in New York for shiva, or mourning period, with my sister. In my grief and distress, I acquiesced. Regrettably, I didn't have the emotional wherewithal to stand up to him at that time, especially since they were *my* kids and, ultimately, not his responsibility. I was embarrassed to tell my family that he demanded I leave. I still hoped to stay married to him and knew they were not fans of his, so I didn't want to makes things worse by telling them the truth.

As I sat shiva by myself at home in Bethesda, I felt lost and deeply ashamed for having abandoned my sister at this important time. Unfortunately, despite my profound and repeated apologies to her over the years, that has affected my relationship with her to this very day.

My fog and depression persisted for several months after my father's death. Wayne and I continued to see Nancy, the couple's therapist, but nothing really changed. I continued to feel constantly criticized by him, even as I resumed our physical relationship, which began to feel more like a job than a pleasure.

I decided to seek bereavement therapy for the loss of my father, which had naturally brought up the pain of my mother's death as well. I contacted the Jewish Social Services Agency, which offered counseling on a sliding scale basis, and was assigned to a social worker named Beth, a smart, assertive, and compassionate woman in her forties.

Beth and I began weekly sessions to address issues of grief and loss but these sessions eventually morphed into examining my marriage to Wayne. With her keen mind and astute observations, I came to the realization that I was in an emotionally abusive marriage, something I had worked very hard to suppress for the sake of keeping the stability of my home intact. We worked on my feelings of guilt regarding my children, who had been through hell already in the three years it took for their father and me to get divorced. I shared my anguish regarding my son's autism, along with the pressure I felt to keep the status quo, especially for his sake.

I learned that this was a story I told myself in order to rationalize staying with Wayne. The truth was that by then, Adam was mostly with his father anyway. Elana continued dividing her time equally between both households. Beth awakened me to the reality that it didn't serve either of my children to stay in an emotionally destructive relationship for the sake of their so-called stability.

As my therapy continued, I began to emerge from my denial but faced the new stress of trying to decide what to do. I was reluctant to shake up my life and that of my children yet again. By then, our first anniversary was right around the corner. In an effort to improve things between us, Wayne suggested that we take a trip to the Bahamas to celebrate. I was reluctant since it would be expensive, given his penchant for fancy vacations. He suggested that we stay at a casino hotel, which offered a "deal," as most casinos do.

Wayne knew his way around casinos all too well. He begged me to let him gamble again, since he had been "such a good boy" and had abstained from gambling, at my insistence, for the last two years. Prior to that, he'd gambled extensively, and, before his bankruptcy, he had gambled feverishly in order to try to salvage his former business. I knew how destructive his addiction was and told him that I would live with him only if he quit. He had agreed. Now he was asking for permission to resume an unhealthy practice. He pleaded that it was "only for this trip." I reluctantly agreed.

We flew down to Nassau and checked into the Atlantis, a luxury hotel and casino situated on the beach. That evening, we dined in one of most exclusive restaurants on the island. Despite the lavish environment, I was unable to enjoy myself. Wayne excused himself after dinner so that he could go to the casino while I stayed in the room and watched a movie. I had no interest in gambling myself. He returned around midnight in a manic state, laden with gifts: a Movado watch, a Chanel handbag, and a Hermes silk scarf.

"Can we afford this?" I asked.

"No problem," he assured me. "I'm on a roll and bought these things from my winnings. Mind if I go back down?" I wasn't sure what to believe but was tired and ready to go to sleep.

"Fine," I said. "Just please make sure to get some rest yourself."

I woke up the next morning with a start. It was clear that Wayne hadn't been to bed. I threw on some sweats and went downstairs where I found him at the blackjack table drinking black coffee.

"What's going on?" I asked.

"Everything's fine," he said. "I was just having too much fun to stop. I'm only down by a few hundred dollars, so I want to keep going. Why don't we have some breakfast, and I'll get back to it while you go to the pool?"

I felt so disgusted that I didn't even want to eat with him. "No thanks. I'm not hungry yet. I'll see you at the pool later," I responded and left the casino.

Furious about how things were turning out, I went back to the room. I spent the morning by myself and was only joined by Wayne later that afternoon after he had gotten a few hours of sleep and was ready to start again. We managed to have a civil dinner together that evening, but he knew I was angry and continued to try to appease me by suggesting more shopping, which I had lost interest in entirely. We toasted to our first year of marriage, but I knew in my heart that there wouldn't be another.

We sat in stony silence for the majority of our flight home. It felt as if his gambling on the trip had triggered his old addiction and brought out the very worst in him. When we got back to the house, we settled in and went downstairs to our family room to relax and watch TV. Wayne asked me not to tell anyone that he had gambled again. I was uncomfortable with that request and told him so. He gave me a terrifying look that I had never seen before, which caused a visceral fear in me. I hurriedly left the room, but, to my horror, he chased me up two flights of stairs to our bedroom, where I tried to close the door on him. We struggled, and he pushed the door open. The rest of what happened seemed to take place in slow motion. He grabbed me, threw me on the bed, slapped me in the face twice, and, as I recoiled in a fetal position, kicked me several times in the back. He then grabbed a stool from my vanity, threw it at me while screaming profanities, and stormed out, proclaiming that he wasn't coming back.

I was stunned and in total shock. Thank goodness my kids hadn't been home to witness this incident. I called my therapist and left a message. She called right back and talked me through steps to ensure my safety. Although I was shaking like a leaf, I was able to take down the information she gave me about filing a protection order to keep him out of the house, which I resolved to do the following morning.

I struggled to make sense of it all. How had this happened to me? Ironically, I had actually been educated and trained in domestic violence during an internship at the Philadelphia district attorney's office while I was a student at Penn. I had worked there full time over the summer of my junior year interviewing and providing legal options to victims of domestic abuse. I had spent my Saturday nights at the police administration building filing emergency protection orders. Most often the complainants would reconcile with their attackers and drop the charges come Monday morning, which always frustrated me to no end. I had studied the cycle of violence in my training and knew that the next stage typically involved profound remorse from the perpetrator, which caused most victims to accept their attackers' apology and try to pick up the pieces of the relationship.

The next day, when Wayne called to say he had gone to a motel the previous night and that he was dreadfully sorry and wanted to come home, I was prepared. I told him in no uncertain terms that he was not going to set foot in the house again and if he tried to come back, I'd file charges against him. He did his best to soften me up, but he could hear the resolve in my trembling voice and realized I wasn't backing down. I told him that I'd work out a time for him to retrieve his things, with police supervision if necessary, and he needed to leave the key and find another place to live immediately. He complied with my demands, packed his clothes, and left the key, along with several gifts I had given him, just to make a point. I immediately changed the locks in the house. I called Howard and asked him to keep the kids a few days longer so that I could take the time I needed to pull myself together.

I fantasized that this incident was a blessing in disguise and that it had been my mother, rather than Wayne, slapping me in the face in order to wake me up to the reality of my situation. I was then tasked with the agonizing job of informing my kids that Wayne and I were over. I was at a loss as to how to present this and sought guidance from my therapist, who advised me how to talk to them. I was heartsick, but, to my tremendous relief, they seemed to accept this much more easily than I had anticipated. I didn't tell them that Wayne had hurt me, only that we had had a bad argument and that I had decided that we needed to go our separate ways.

Perhaps they had sensed that I was becoming increasingly unhappy, or they had begun to feel uncomfortable around Wayne themselves. Either way, they seemed to make a decent adjustment, each in their own way. Elana was curious as to what kind of argument would have ended an entire marriage. I didn't want to disclose the gory details but explained that a line had been crossed in our relationship and that there didn't seem to be a way back, which was the honest truth. Adam didn't react outwardly but understood full well what was happening.

Not long after Wayne left, we went out to one of our favorite self-service Chinese-Japanese restaurants in Rockville, Maryland, where they gave each order a number and then delivered it to the table. The number for the kids' Chinese food was thirty-three and my sushi order number was three. Adam looked at both numbers on the table and said, "Thirty-three and three. We used to be four. Now we're three." That simple statement summed it all up. I felt as if a dagger had been stuck into my heart.

I tried as best as I could to pick up the pieces in the aftermath of that horrible night. I informed Nancy, our couples therapist, about what had occurred. She asked to meet, and, to my amazement, this news did not surprise her. She told me that her assessment of

Wayne's ability to function in a healthy relationship was extremely low. She felt that he was "doing a sales job" on her all along. Then she coined a phrase that startled me. She said he was a "textbook abusive personality" and, in addition, likely had a chemical imbalance as well as a personality disorder.

"Wow," I thought, "I suppose I was doomed from the very beginning. All that therapy for nothing."

Beth, my individual therapist, listened sympathetically and without judgment. She referred me to the Montgomery County Abused Persons Program and suggested that I work with a specialist there and join a therapy group. I decided I needed to do everything I could to come to terms with what had happened and to take responsibility for the decisions that had led me to that point.

The work was painful yet necessary. In addition to the specialized therapy, I read everything I could on abusive personality syndrome, which was eye opening. In my group therapy, everyone told their particular story, but it felt as if everyone had described the same man across the socioeconomic spectrum: controlling, insecure, quick to anger, and potentially violent. I felt humiliated to be among this group of victims and determined to make sure something like this would never happen again.

Eventually, Wayne rented a studio apartment nearby. After renting a room in a house for three months, he began another campaign to reconcile with me, pulling out all the stops with apologies, gifts, promises to travel together, and financial assistance to make my life easier. Of course, I was skeptical, knowing that this was part of the cycle of violence and that, unless he got treatment, history would repeat itself. But we were still married, and part of me still loved him, despite the trauma I had suffered.

Carol, the abuse specialist I began seeing, said that it was possible to salvage our marriage, but only if he immersed himself into intensive, specialized therapy, which would take time. I was willing to give it time since my commitment to my marriage still meant something to me. I told him that I would not live with him but would consider dating him on three conditions: 1) he get specialized therapy for abuse, 2) he see a psychopharmacologist and get on medication for his chemical imbalance, and 3) we seek the legal services of my former divorce attorney and obtain a separation agreement, which would protect me financially in case we proceeded to divorce. He agreed. He acknowledged that he had made a horrible mistake and that there wasn't anything he wouldn't do to get back together with me. I then explained to my kids that Wayne was receiving treatment and that I therefore owed it to our marriage to give him a chance. They seemed to accept this.

True to his word, he enrolled in therapy, got on medication, and offered me a very generous financial settlement in the event things didn't work out. Meanwhile, he sent me a monthly check to cover household expenses, which he had shared with me before he left.

Wayne was forced to confront the fact that he was an abuser and would share what he had learned in therapy with me as he went along. He told me that he owed me a huge debt of gratitude for forcing him to address his very significant problems. I learned that he had witnessed his own father physically abuse his mother throughout his childhood, something no one else in the family shared with me, even after I disclosed what had transpired between us. I began to understand why he was so troubled, which gave me a deeper appreciation for the root of his problems and the compassion to forgive him. A glimmer of hope began to emerge that perhaps he could be rehabilitated.

That spring, I planned to take Elana to Israel as a post bat mitzvah gift. It was my dream to introduce her to the country where I was born and about which she had studied extensively in primary Jewish day school. I enrolled us in a United Jewish Communities trip geared toward introducing bar- and bat-mitzvah-aged kids to Israel for the first time. It included a ten-day tour of the country as well as a bar/bat mitzvah ceremony in the ruins of an ancient synagogue. I had saved for quite some time to be able to afford the best experience possible.

After asking Elana's permission, I invited Wayne to join us on that trip. He would pay his own way. By then, he had kept all of his promises and demonstrated his commitment to his treatment. He was in weekly therapy, saw a psychiatrist monthly, and was on medication, which seemed effective. We had been seeing each other a few times a week, either at his place or out with the kids. I thought it would be nice for him to also experience Israel for the first time himself, but he declined the invitation, expressing no interest whatsoever in Israel, which surprised but didn't really disappoint me. "It will be a mother-daughter trip, which is even better," I thought, as I went about planning for just the two of us.

Wayne seemed to resent the fact that I was going anyway, as if he'd expected me to give up on the idea if he didn't come along. Due in large part to my own therapy, I didn't really care whether my trip upset him or not. I was excited to be going. As the time approached, he offered to drive us to the airport. I accepted.

When we were done packing up the car and got settled inside, I could tell that something was off with him. He turned what should have been a happy ride to the airport into the opposite experience, with his anger and resentment at our leaving boiling over. I didn't react and tried to put a brave face on for Elana's sake, but after he dropped us off and we cleared security and boarded the plane, I was in tears. Elana looked at me and said, "Mom, he hasn't changed one bit." "Out of the mouths of babes," I thought. It was good that we were going away. I'd have a change of scenery and much time to think things over.

The trip with Elana was fabulous and gave us a lifetime of memories to cherish. I felt grounded and happy being in Israel, where I could communicate with friends and family in Hebrew. Elana fell in love with Israel, which delighted me. I knew this was the beginning of her connection to my beloved country, which I hoped would continue over her lifetime.

I did my own soul searching on that trip and prayed for guidance to do the right thing going forward. Coming home was difficult. I didn't know what to expect. Wayne waited for us at the airport, this time upbeat and happy to see us. He had called a few times while we were away, but with the time difference and our travel schedule, we had barely spoken. The plan was to drop Elana off at her father's house before returning to mine.

Elana and I hugged goodbye for the time being, leaving Wayne and me alone for the first time in weeks. He apologized for his behavior when we left and said that in our absence, he had realized how unfair his resentment about the trip had been. He was glad it had been such a success. I appreciated his acknowledgment.

We got back to my house and made love for the first time in a very long time. The physical part of our relationship had always been strong, and that connection was still there. Afterward, he patted me on my butt and said, "Time to get back to the gym!"

I was deeply insulted and responded, "Why would you say something like that to me *now*, of all times?"

"I didn't mean anything by it," he responded defensively. "I just meant that you had gotten out of your gym routine with the trip and all, and it would be good to get back to it. You know I think you're beautiful."

"Wayne," I said, "there's not a woman alive who wouldn't have had a problem with that comment, especially given the timing."

I got up, dressed, and told him that I'd like some time to myself to get settled. I then asked him to leave. He obliged, all the while defending his comment by saying that he didn't mean anything and I had blown the entire thing way out of proportion.

I stewed all night about Wayne's remark and, by the next day, had made a decision. Jet-lagged or not, I was done. That comment was the tipping point for me. When he called the next day, I told him that I had thought things over and decided that our marriage was over for good.

He was stunned. "Over that silly comment?" he asked.

"Wayne," I said, "I've thought things over. Honestly, if after everything we've been through and all your therapy, if this is the best you can do, it's simply not good enough," I said. There was no dissuading me. My experience in Israel, along with Elana's comment, had steeled me for what I knew in my heart was the right decision.

After my final rejection of Wayne, he decided that he was finished in our community and moved to the Miami area where a good friend of his lived. I was happy to see him go. I could now be spared the awkwardness of running into him. I was no longer heartbroken, having crossed a threshold in my own recovery. I made sure to have my children say their goodbyes to him, as my therapist had recommended, so they, too, could close that chapter in a healthy way. They were neither surprised nor heartbroken, which was a tremendous relief. Elana actually said that she was proud of me, both for trying my best and for walking away from what she knew deep down was a bad situation. Her insight and sensitivity for such a young girl touched me deeply. "I must have done something right among all this mess," I thought and then counted my blessings.

My family was relieved that Wayne was out of my life. My sister congratulated me on "waking up from my coma." I knew it would be a very long time before I got involved with anyone else. It was time to be alone and focus on my own healing and continued recovery.

# CHAPTER TWENTY-FOUR

## Recovery and Beyond

*M*adeline was a bit of a late bloomer. A tall, athletic girl growing up, she'd always felt awkward and self-conscious around her high school peers. Eventually, she attended an Ivy League university and earned a master's degree in genetics, hoping to begin a career as a genetic counselor to couples facing infertility. Although she had blossomed into quite an attractive woman, at age forty-two, she still struggled with low self-esteem. I was immediately impressed with Madeline and wanted to help her meet and marry the man of her dreams.

We established a great working relationship from the start. I introduced her to three men, who all liked her, but she didn't warm up to any of them. Then someone in my social circle referred me to Owen, a self-employed entrepreneur, who, at age forty-five, had never been married. Based on his description, he sounded like a potential match for Madeline. He eagerly agreed to meet with me and was open and forthcoming with me about his life, his past relationships, and his desire to settle down. He explained how he had started his business and was working

185

feverishly to take his electronics company public after becoming more successful than he ever thought possible.

I liked Owen and felt that he had much to offer intellectually, emotionally, and financially. I also had the sense that he and Madeline would have good chemistry between them, which turned out to be true, with a vengeance. They hit it off beautifully. Owen had been dating someone casually for a while before meeting Madeline but quickly ended that relationship to focus on dating Madeline exclusively.

Owen was the perfect boyfriend to Madeline, who had never experienced the kind of affection and support she got from Owen. He was smitten, and his enthusiasm was hard for Madeline to resist. Within six months, they were engaged. They married six months later. I was delighted to list them among my successes.

Only a few short weeks into their marriage, however, things began to change. Owen, once totally available to Madeline, began working more and more until Madeline began to feel neglected. When she expressed any concerns on her part, he would quickly shut her down, calling her "ungrateful" for his emerging success. Slowly, her happiness began to fade, and she found herself the victim of emotional and eventually verbal abuse on his part toward her. Their marriage quickly deteriorated, and within just six months of their wedding, they separated.

Madeline was devastated and felt that she could no longer remain in the DC area, given all the connections to Owen, which were a painful reminder of what she had suffered. She therefore moved back to her hometown of Cleveland, where she took a job she was overqualified for, just to give her the opportunity to be near her parents and to heal from the trauma of her marriage. Her move allowed her to get her through the divorce process without being exposed to him as well.

Two years later, Madeline was divorced and beginning to tire of her job in Cleveland. She had gotten stronger and had begun to feel as if she had given up a part of herself by leaving the DC area because of Owen. After encouragement from her family and a talented therapist who helped her work through her divorce, Madeline began job hunting in DC and was fortunate to receive a terrific offer in her field. She moved back to DC and resumed her life as a single woman.

Madeline contacted me when she returned and engaged my services once again. I was touched that she trusted me enough to work with me again, especially since I had been the one to introduce her to Owen in the first place. She explained that in her work in therapy, she came to realize why she had been so vulnerable to Owen, who was brilliant at hiding his darker side until she had fully committed to him by marrying him. Of course, this story was not unfamiliar to me after my experience with Wayne.

In my second round of matchmaking for Madeline, I coached her to try to avoid her tendency to blame herself for not recognizing how toxic a man Owen had been. I shared my own story with her, as well as several books and articles dealing with abuse, explaining that women like us aren't primed to look for or accustomed to dealing with someone with that pathology. "Many other intelligent women have fallen prey to that type of man, and it is to our credit," I explained, "that we got out quickly, once we 'saw the writing on the wall.'"

Unfortunately, I did not find Madeline a second husband during our second contract together, but she met several very decent men through me, who helped her recognize her strengths and further heal from the trauma of her divorce. She and I remained friends for several years afterward, and I recently learned, through a mutual acquaintance, that she began dating someone seriously. Shortly after hearing this news, I happened to run into her with her new boyfriend, and she seemed very happy and comfortable with him. He struck me as a very decent fellow, and I was relieved to see her in what looked like a stable relationship with a man who seemed worthy of her. We shared a private moment where I expressed my pleasure at seeing her with someone who seemed nice and very devoted to her. The following day, she e-mailed me, telling me how wonderful it was to run into me and that she felt it was "fate" having her new boyfriend meet her matchmaker's approval.

## CHAPTER TWENTY-FIVE

# Half a Century Wiser

*I*n the months preceding my fiftieth birthday, I decided to celebrate this milestone by treating myself to a spa getaway, which had come highly recommended. Rancho La Puerta, a retreat in the Mexican countryside, offered three organic meals a day and a wide array of activities, including hiking, exercise and dance classes, along with specialized workshops in art, photography, music, and other crafts. In addition, they had a full range of spa services so guests could work out and then get pampered, as desired. I saved my money so I could afford private accommodations there, in addition to the round-trip airfare to San Diego, where Rancho La Puerta guests would be driven by charter bus across the border to Tecate, Mexico.

About two months prior to my trip, out of the blue, I received a call from Gary, my former college boyfriend and first love. Gary and I had stayed in touch approximately every five to seven years. He knew that his college friend Howard and I had married. In fact, Gary had actually gotten together with us twice, once in DC, and once in Los Angeles, where Gary had moved after graduating from Penn.

Gary had started his own film editing company while living in LA. It was there where he met and married Pam, a Scientologist, who had gotten him involved in the church as well. I was eight months pregnant with Adam when we got together as couples in LA. Howard and I had traveled there on business for Howard's job at that time. We arranged to have dinner together, where we met Pam for the first time. I was shocked. Her dull affect was completely flat compared to Gary's effusive personality. I chalked this up to her involvement in Scientology and was relieved it hadn't affected Gary similarly.

We met at a local Mexican restaurant over drinks, mine being nonalcoholic due to my pregnancy. Within the first half hour of our meeting, Gary spontaneously shared that he had learned a few years earlier that he was sterile. He and Pam were therefore in the process of trying to adopt a child. This disclosure saddened me, since Gary had always wanted children. He came from a large Catholic family, was one of eight siblings, and had always assumed he'd have a large family of his own. It was especially awkward for me as his former girlfriend, since I was *very* pregnant at the time. Oddly enough, after having a few bites of guacamole, I started feeling funny and had to excuse myself. Once I reached the ladies room, I became violently ill. "Was this psychological or physical?" I wondered. Either way, it was embarrassing. I subsequently learned that I had developed an allergy to avocado, which oddly continues to this day, apparently activated by my pregnancy.

About two years later, Gary flew into DC on business. Howard and I took him out to dinner in Georgetown at our favorite Italian restaurant. As we drove there, we caught up on each other's lives. Gary and Pam had adopted a daughter named Heidi after fostering her for almost two years. Heidi was eight years old when they finally adopted her. She was not an easy child, but they derived a great deal of fulfillment from stepping into her life and took enormous pride in giving her the family life she needed.

I was pleased for him that he had become a dad and was sure he was completely devoted to Heidi. We did not ask him about his involvement in Scientology, since I didn't want to open that can of worms. Both Howard and I viewed Scientology as an unhealthy cult. I never understood how Gary had allowed Pam to indoctrinate him into the church in the first place.

By the time I turned fifty, I had been divorced from Howard for about ten years and learned, through mutual friends, that Gary and Pam had divorced as well. At that juncture, I was delighted to get a call from Gary. Here we were, both single again and talking on the phone after more than ten years without any communication. He told me that he had decided to call because he had seen me on Facebook and couldn't get over how great I looked. I was thrilled to receive that affirmation from him, especially since he had been my first lover. I wondered how he looked as well, and he said that he would e-mail me a photo.

Gary brought me up to date on his life, explaining that the reason for his divorce was that Pam had chosen Scientology over him. He had become increasingly disillusioned with the church's doctrines and chose to disengage. To his credit, I thought, but Pam could not accept this and decided to leave him as a result. Since their divorce, he had been Heidi's primary caregiver. She was now about twenty years old and still in need of a lot of support from both her parents. Pam and Heidi did not get along particularly well, but Gary said that if anything ever happened to him, Pam would step up and be there for Heidi wholeheartedly.

During our conversation, Gary also reported that he'd had some health challenges. He explained that he had suffered a minor heart attack two years earlier and, as a result, had quit smoking, stopped eating meat, and was leading a much healthier and active lifestyle. Gary had always been super thin, so I had a hard time picturing him with a heart condition. He said that he was taking great care of himself now and felt better than ever.

I told Gary about my divorce from Howard and my subsequent debacle with Wayne, and he listened sympathetically. Despite being on my own, I told him I was doing well and, in fact, was planning to be in San Diego briefly on my way to The Ranch (as it was known) in a few months. He sounded excited to hear this and suggested that we meet, offering to take some time off from work, rent a car, and drive down to Tijuana, which was near The Ranch. He knew of The Ranch and suggested that he pick me up and take me around the Mexican wine country. I asked how safe that would be, and he replied that he'd done it before and that he'd only take me to areas he was familiar with. I enthusiastically agreed to his plan.

Gary and I spoke for about an hour more about our jobs, kids, and life in general. Just before ending the conversation, he said, "Leora, before I go, I'd just like to say how sorry I am for the hurt I caused you while we were together."

Touched by his heartfelt apology, I responded, "Gary, you really don't need to apologize. That was so long ago, and we were so young."

"Well, I just wanted to let you know that it's been on my mind all these years," he explained. "You were so wonderful and didn't deserve how I treated you."

"Thanks for telling me that," I replied. "It means a lot to hear you say it. For what it's worth, I forgive you."

Gary paused. Unsure of what else to say, we wrapped up the conversation and finalized our plans to meet. I sat there with the phone, as well as my heart, in my hand for several minutes after we hung up. "Wow," I thought. "He's been carrying around those feelings of guilt for almost thirty years. I must have really left an impression on him, and now, after all this time, he shows up, single, asking for forgiveness. Could this mean another chance for us? Who knows," I thought. "Anything's possible."

When I received Gary's most current photo, I was surprised at how different, but still handsome, he looked. At fifty-one, he had filled out, had a full head of gray hair, and sported a small goatee. I began to daydream about how it would be for us to see each other again. Would it be a reunion of old friends or something more? The romantic in me wanted to believe that fate had intervened to bring us back together after all those years apart.

*The romantic in me wanted to believe that fate had intervened to bring us back together after all those years apart.*

As I prepared for my trip, I was surprised not to have heard from Gary. I wondered whether he might have had a change of heart about seeing me again, or perhaps had met someone new and lost interest in the idea. Either way, his silence puzzled me. I decided not to contact him, so as to allow him to take the lead on our meeting, since he had been the one to suggest it.

I flew directly from Baltimore/Washington International Thurgood Marshall Airport (BWI) to San Diego. On the flight, I sat in the same row as a woman who was the spitting image of a good friend of mine from New York. A man sat between us, so we didn't have the chance to speak to each other during the five-hour flight. When we landed, I headed straight to baggage claim. There she stood, with the same identifying tags I had from The Ranch. "What an odd coincidence," I thought.

We introduced ourselves to each other. Her name was Robin. When she learned my name, she said that she knew of me and my matchmaking business through her friend Carol, a photographer, who had done a photo shoot for my business brochure a few years earlier. Robin further explained that Carol would be her roommate at The Ranch. I was delighted to learn that I would know someone there. Robin then asked if I wanted to sit with her for the two-hour bus ride into Mexico. "This trip is off to a fantastic start," I thought. "I'm not even out of the airport and I've already made a new friend!"

During the trip to The Ranch, I learned all about Robin. She was an artist, living only a few miles from me in Bethesda. She was a sultry brunette just a few years older than me and had been widowed about five years earlier. She had just fallen for a new man, whom she had met online and who had stirred feelings in her for the first time since losing her husband.

I told Robin my story as well. She thought I'd chosen wisely for my fiftieth, since The Ranch was the perfect place to celebrate myself, unwind, and have a great physical and spiritual experience. I also shared my Gary story with her, complete with our breakup, as well as my excitement over our plans to meet later that week.

Carol, who had gotten there earlier, greeted Robin once we arrived. She was surprised and delighted to see me there as well, as was I to see her. Now I had two friends to hang out with that week!

True to Robin's word, The Ranch was magnificent. It stood at the foot of a mountain and was landscaped beautifully. It was springtime, and everything was in full bloom. The place looked like a Disney movie set. I had my own individual cottage, which was spacious and decorated in Aztec style, with handmade rugs and beautifully designed lamps, vases, and pictures throughout. Outside the picture window was a stunning view of the mountain.

I was thrilled to be there and to share the experience with both Carol and Robin. In between our classes, spa appointments, and hikes, we had all of our meals together, but despite my newfound friends and busy schedule, I couldn't get Gary out of my mind. I found it odd that I hadn't heard from him since my arrival at The Ranch.

Two days into my stay, I decided to check if Gary had been in touch. Guests were discouraged from going online, so we didn't have Wi-Fi in our rooms and had to use the computer room at The Ranch to access e-mail. When I opened mine, to my horror,

I saw a message from an unknown sender with the subject line "Memorial service for Gary." I read further and learned that he had died of a heart attack two days before I left for California. I sat there stunned, tears running down my cheeks. I tried to digest this new reality. "Gary dead at fifty-one . . . How was that possible? And just as our paths were about to cross again!" I thought. I ran our last conversation over and over again in my head. Perhaps he'd had a sixth sense that his death was imminent and reached out to make amends with me before it was too late? What an incredible gift he had bestowed upon me! I sat there and cried for what had happened and for what was never to be.

## CHAPTER TWENTY-SIX

# In Sickness and in Health

*L*eo and Rhonda were in their late sixties when I introduced
them. She was divorced with grown children and had
been on her own for over ten years. She was a stylish and elegant
woman who enjoyed fashion and looked more like a New Yorker
than a native Washingtonian, despite the fact that she had grown
up in Chevy Chase. I recruited Leo to meet her through a scout of
mine who had met him at a singles' dance. He was a partner in a
prestigious law firm and looked and acted the part.

When I sat down with Leo to vet him on Rhonda's behalf,
I was surprised to discover a deeply emotional man under his
"alpha male" exterior. He quickly warmed to me and confided
in me about the painful loss of his marriage in the midst of his
recovery from a near-fatal illness. He had been diagnosed with
leukemia when he was in his fifties and on top of his game, both
professionally and personally. His marriage of twenty-five years
had been fairly solid, and he had enjoyed the fruits of his success

by providing his family with an enviable home, lavish vacations, and private school educations for his two children.

Leo's diagnosis came as a complete shock to his then-wife, Valerie. She could not wrap her mind around the fact that Leo was no longer her pillar of strength but vulnerable and in need of empathy and support for what he was about to endure. Sadly, Leo learned that once he was no longer the "dream husband" he had been to Valerie, she became resentful and was unable to rally on his behalf. This was a huge blow to Leo, who was having enough trouble adjusting to his treatments without the additional heartache of discovering that his wife was not the woman he'd always presumed her to be. Slowly, they became increasingly estranged from each other during a time when he needed her more than ever.

Miraculously, Leo survived; however, his marriage to Valerie did not. It turned out to be a very public and contentious divorce, which embittered Leo and put him off of marriage altogether for quite some time. When he met Rhonda, however, he was able to recognize the loving woman she was, and a part of him that had previously shut down opened up to her. For the first time in decades, he experienced the love he had longed for with Valerie, and his former unhappiness dissolved as his relationship with Rhonda deepened.

They moved in together after six months, got engaged, and three months later, held an intimate June wedding ceremony in the back yard of the house they had purchased together. Their home was the perfect venue for the wedding. It was a showcase of style and warmth and a reflection of their shared tastes. Between them, they had five adult children who rejoiced for them, despite their misgivings at the beginning of their relationship.

They were blissfully happy for six years when tragically, Leo's illness returned. They had known that there was a risk that this could happen but had moved forward anyway. This time, however,

Leo had the love and devotion of Rhonda, who singlehandedly committed herself to his recovery. When it eventually became clear that he wasn't going to make it, she became his "angel of mercy" who loved him unconditionally until the very end.

"Perhaps I was spared this agony by never meeting Gary," I reflected, when I heard about Leo's passing. While I was never given the chance, Rhonda had courageously taken the risk of marrying Leo, due to the strength of her feelings toward him.

At his memorial service, Rhonda told me that despite this devastating loss, she felt that she had made the right choice. Their marriage of six years had been the happiest time of her life, and she still had hope that one day she'd have someone to love and care for her when her time came. I was reminded of how extraordinary a woman she was and wished the same for her as well.

After a two-year period of mourning, Rhonda returned to me as a client. Unfortunately, lightning didn't strike twice for her. While she will always cherish the love she and Leo had shared, she appreciated the opportunity to "get out there" and feel alive once again.

## CHAPTER TWENTY-SEVEN

# Building a Foundation

*L*earning to trust again was a challenge. It had been twelve years since my second divorce, which was finalized in April 2000. I threw myself a birthday/divorce party on the weekend following the court hearing that finalized my divorce from Wayne. I had foolishly taken his last name, due to pressure from him, and was happy to revert to my former name, as it was consistent with my children's and the name under which I established my business. It was time to celebrate my freedom from my former marriage and start a new, hopefully better, chapter.

During the twelve years between my second divorce and meeting Jim, I continued to run my business and raise my children on a half-time basis, since I had joint custody with their father. I also resumed practicing law in a new specialty of child protection. I did a fair amount of online dating during that time, since my options for meeting men were limited as a matchmaker. I learned how to navigate various dating sites, which included Jdate, Match, and Plenty of Fish.

My experiences dating online ran the gamut. Dan, a Jewish South African with whom I was involved for eleven months, turned out to be a major jerk, and a commitment phobic one at that. Rick, a twice-divorced Methodist fellow, developed an obsession with a woman he had dropped when we first got together after dating me for eight months. I then dated a Jewish fellow named Brad who worked for the FBI and who proved, after only four months, to be a pathological liar, the most egregious lie being that he was *actually* divorced after a five-year separation. I also dated a Jewish man from Baltimore named Mitch. We became engaged after two years, but that ended after he refused to set a wedding date or move in together like we had planned once we got engaged.

After all the work I had done in therapy, I had been determined not to make another mistake. I was the one to walk away from those other relationships after realizing that none of them were men I could "go the distance" with, which was my goal. Despite the disappointments, I found it empowering to have developed the capacity to cut my losses so I could continue to search for the right man, a goal I was determined to meet.

Meeting Jim was a revelation. He had his own issues, just as I had mine, but he was a fundamentally decent and loving man, who had practiced being a good husband for over twenty years. He was also the smartest and funniest man I had ever met, and he stimulated me both intellectually and emotionally, something I hadn't experienced with my former husbands or beaus, except for Ian, who had set the "gold standard." Jim was the first man I had met who even came close to possessing and actually exceeding the qualities that had attracted me to Ian.

Our courtship was romantic, fun, and exciting. We shared a passion for music, movies, travel, and eclectic dining, and we never ran out of things to do. We couldn't get enough of each other. We were also lucky to be living only fifteen minutes apart, so we fairly quickly fell into a pattern of spending every weekend and several nights during the week together. I was happy for the first time in a long time. After only four months together, my instincts told me that he was a "keeper," but it was too soon to say for sure.

That summer, we decided to take a ten-day trip abroad to a destination where neither of us had been before. I had always dreamed of visiting Istanbul, Turkey, especially after I had learned that the late John F. Kennedy Jr., whom I had greatly admired, had chosen it as his honeymoon destination. I longed to visit the Hagia Sofia and the Blue Mosque, take a boat ride up the Bosporous Straight, tour their world-famous museums, shop, and dine on their Mediterranean cuisine. Our trip would be hectic with everything I wanted to see, so I suggested we pair it with a restful, week-long beach experience on the nearby island of Santorini, Greece, which we were both familiar with from travel brochures and had dreamed of traveling to.

Jim jumped at the chance to visit both of those places. During his marriage to Cynthia, he had done almost no international traveling, so was eager to change that. We happily set about planning our trip. Both of us had major skills in that area. I was the daughter of a travel agent, and Jim was an accomplished researcher himself. He found both of the hotels, which were unique and reasonably priced. I was delighted to relinquish my usual role of "cruise director" and defer to someone who could competently handle the arrangements.

Istanbul lived up to its reputation. It was exciting, educational, and action packed. From there, we flew to Santorini, a magical oasis on the Mediterranean Sea.

While in Santorini, Jim surprised me with a gorgeous blue gem and pearl bracelet we had admired in a shop window. This touched me deeply. He had already been so generous in Istanbul by treating me to several pieces of jewelry and a silk scarf. Having used my best bargaining skills, I, in turn, bought him a leather jacket at the Grand Bazaar. I came by those skills honestly, as I had grown up observing my father masterfully negotiate with every merchant on the avenue where we lived in Brooklyn. Jim appeared very impressed.

It was a heavenly week, the perfect mixture of rest and relaxation, passion, and adventure. We took a Santorini wine tour and then rented a car and explored the island, utilizing Jim's expert driving skills. We also took a catamaran tour of the island's beaches, swam to the mineral hot springs, and enjoyed the view of the island from the surface below.

Spending every waking moment together forced us to learn more about each other's habits, rhythms, and idiosyncrasies. We spent endless hours talking, often getting lost in deep conversation. We enjoyed our time together so much that we never wanted to leave and even joked about dropping out of society altogether in favor of my slinging feta cheese as a waitress and Jim driving a tourist bus around the island.

On our last night there, we dined at one of the nicest restaurants on the island, which was attached to a very exclusive resort. The restaurant was situated on a floating platform on the water. It was the perfect finale to our island experience. Toward the end of the meal, I looked Jim in the eye and asked, "So, after this trip, do you love me even more?" fully expecting him to say yes. To my surprise, he blushed but didn't respond. I was crushed and embarrassed to feel the tears welling up in my eyes.

"You had to go and ask that question," I told myself. You should know by now, as a trained lawyer, never to ask a question you're not prepared to hear the answer to," I chided myself internally. "Why couldn't you leave well enough alone?"

Seeing how mortified I was, Jim took my hand and explained. "Leora, this has been a very intense experience. I haven't been with anyone like this in a very long time and will need some time to process it all. It's been a trip of a lifetime, but it's also been stressful for me to adjust to someone new. We have very different styles, which became obvious in several situations during our time together. It's not that I don't love you, it's just that this will take time."

"Did we make a mistake by taking this trip too soon?" I asked, as the tears began to flow.

"No, sweetheart," he responded. "We did take a risk, though, which, in my opinion, has been anything but a mistake. It's been amazing. Just give me time."

Then I broke the tension by mimicking one of our favorite TV characters, a touchstone for us both and for baby boomers in general. Ralph Kramden, from *The Honeymooners*, would, in his self-deprecating way, say what "A BIG MOUTH" he had. We laughed together and kissed sweetly as he wiped my tears away. I knew then that Jim had the depth of character I had always looked for in a partner. He was the kind of man who would always level with me, whether I liked it or not, and could be trusted to tell me the truth, something that meant so much more to me than being placated by compliments. "I have to be patient," I thought, "but this relationship might just be the payoff I've been praying for."

About two months later, we were having breakfast at our local diner and the subject of our "future" came up. Jim looked at me point-blank and said, "You do know where this is heading, right? I'm not interested in finding a roommate. I'm interested in marriage." I blushed as my heart skipped a beat. This was the first time he had actually used the "M" word. I knew by then that Jim did not mince words and that he meant whatever he said. This was both reassuring and scary for me at the same time. I didn't necessarily need to be married again, but I wanted a committed relationship with someone whom I could count on as a life partner. At the same time, I believed in marriage and aspired to the kind of marriage I had witnessed between several couples I had been close to in my life. It was a level of commitment and a form of permanency I craved, but I was also terrified of making another mistake. I shared my conflicting emotions with Jim, who understood and reassuringly took my hand and said, "No pressure at all. Let's just take things one step at a time." I was okay with leaving it there.

One morning when we were staying at Jim's house in Potomac, he woke up from a dream agitated and upset. When I asked him what was wrong, he told me not to panic but that he'd had a dream about Cynthia and was feeling as if he was "betraying" her by being with me. I stayed calm but, given my natural neurotic tendencies, couldn't help but panic internally. "What if he can't do this?" I thought. "Maybe, despite all his reassurances, he really hasn't gotten over her and never will."

"Have you thought about going back into therapy?" I asked.

After Cynthia's death, Jim had received a year of weekly grief therapy and had also been part of a bereavement group. "Perhaps he needs a refresher," I thought, as I struggled to come up with a solution.

Jim shook his head. "I don't think so," he said. "I'm not looking for a quick fix. I truly think this is a question of time. It's like throwing a pebble into a lake. The ripples gradually diminish. I think that's all this is about. I just needed to share this with you and to have you listen sympathetically."

I had become increasingly uncomfortable in Jim's house as our relationship progressed. At first, I had been reluctant to even sleep in the bed he had shared with Cynthia, even though he had gotten a new mattress before I even came on the scene. At that time, he had understood my reluctance but said that it would be wonderful to "have some joy in his bed" after sleeping alone for so many years. That idea resonated with me.

I wanted to comfort and nurture him. But over time, being in his environment began to weigh on me. I was surrounded by reminders of Cynthia. Her pictures were displayed on his fridge and in a large framed photo on his desk near his computer, where we often sat together. While he would move the picture on his desk when I asked, he had also hung three large framed collages from her work as a graphic designer in the dining area. I found these images somewhat disturbing. In the guest room where I kept my things, three of her straw hats were displayed on the dresser.

As a Jewish girl involved with a widower, I began to feel like I was living a scene out of *Fiddler on the Roof*. My thoughts conjured up the dream sequence where Fruma-Sarah, the late wife of Lazer Wolf, the butcher, to whom Tevye's older daughter had been promised, comes from the grave to curse their engagement. I knew the whole idea was ridiculous, but I still couldn't shake the feeling that Cynthia's spirit was haunting me. I suggested that we spend more time at my place, where there were no reminders of any previous relationships. Of course, I understood that, for Jim's sake, it was unfair to expect him to always be the one to pack a bag. I told him that I longed for a time when we might have our own place together so we could start fresh.

As the holidays approached, just nine months into our relationship, we encountered some more challenges as old memories came up for Jim and he struggled to reconcile them with his new life with me. I had tried to manage my own emotions every time Jim would speak of Cynthia, which was too frequent for my liking. After all, I had been through two prior marriages and had been very careful not to speak of my exes, except for issues that were still present involving my children and by necessity with their father. While I understood that this was baggage that I brought to the relationship myself, I viewed it differently. I had no choice but to deal with my ex, who was very much alive, while in my mind, Jim *did* have a choice about bringing his late wife up between us. Perhaps that was unfair on my part.

When I dug deeper and looked at the reality of my situation, however, I had to admit that I was extremely lucky. He did not have children nor did he have a living ex-spouse whom I would have had to deal with, as he did with mine. He was professionally accomplished, financially solid, and emotionally available. What more could I ask for? I realized that the many years I had struggled with other men had caused me to always be "waiting for the other shoe to drop" in my relationships.

It was time to face those insecurities rather than impose them onto Jim. I had no reason to doubt his devotion to me, and if I had to live with the "ghost" of his late wife, I could handle that, as long as Jim was careful not to rub it in my face.

The true test came that Christmas. Jim planned to visit Cynthia's family in Santa Fe, which had been his annual tradition even after she passed away. She came from a large, very loving family, who all gathered each year at her mother's house for the holiday. Since Jim had grown up as an only child, he looked forward to being with her family, who had embraced him as their own from the time he and Cynthia had gotten together. Since I didn't celebrate Christmas, I understood and accepted his need to have that experience and to reconnect with his in-laws. I was prepared to be apart from him for the holiday weekend.

To my surprise, Jim invited me to join him for Christmas in Santa Fe. I felt torn. This could actually serve as a form of "aversion therapy" for me. I was being asked to immerse myself in the very situation I struggled to handle. My instinct was to say no, but, as I thought about it further, I realized that his invitation was the ultimate compliment. He wanted his adopted family to meet and know me, perhaps to even give him their blessing, before going forward with me. But could I handle it, and was it even a good idea? It would be like walking into the lion's den. There was no way of knowing how the family would feel about my being there. I asked myself when had I ever shied away from a challenge and mustered all my reserves. "I can do this," I told myself. "Besides, I want to share Jim's holiday with him, and if he wants me along, I'm prepared to take that leap of faith, just as he's taken it with me."

I stood nervously alongside Jim at the front door of the Nelson family home in Santa Fe. Margo, the eldest sister, opened the door, gave Jim a hug, and turned to me and said, "Wow, you're brave!" She understood and was calling it for what it was.

It felt good to be among enlightened and progressive people. As Jim had assured me, the family turned out to be wonderful. They embraced me warmly and expressed genuine happiness for Jim. Despite my apprehension, our three days there were both fun and meaningful. I felt comfortable enough to go on a hike with Jim's brother-in-law, Brett, a very warm and friendly chemist, and his German shepard, Millie. I also made sure to give Jim time to himself with the family by exploring the nearby mall to shop for my kids.

The visit was a big success. When it came time to leave and we were saying our goodbyes, Margo pulled Jim aside and said, "You lucked out. Don't screw it up." According to Jim, that was the ultimate praise, as Margo was not one to hand out compliments lightly. As we drove away, I was happy and relieved that everything had worked out so well. I knew we had achieved another milestone in our relationship.

## CHAPTER TWENTY-EIGHT

# Set Your Differences Aside

*J*ustin was one of my best clients. He was a handsome, divorced, fifty-two-year-old lobbyist who had been inundated with dating prospects since his divorce. Everyone from his colleagues to the neighbors presented him with fabulous prospects, but he was too busy and selective to sift through them all. He also worried that it would be too awkward to meet a woman through people he knew well, in the event that things didn't work out.

During our initial consultation, he shared his history with me. The mother of his children suddenly passed away a few years after their divorce. He was therefore more like a widower, as far as his teenage children were concerned, and was seeking a woman who'd blend in with his children and be an effective stepparent, which wouldn't be easy given what they'd been through. He also had strong political views as a liberal Democrat and wanted to meet a woman with similar values, or one who would at least be accepting of his.

I got to work on Justin's behalf and first introduced him to a forty-five-year-old attorney with two children. She was a partner in a litigation firm and had the strength of character I knew could work for Justin. I turned out to be right about Justin's interest in her. He was captivated by her beauty, intelligence, and assertiveness, but, unfortunately, she didn't feel similarly after their three dates together. The next referral was to a very attractive forty-eight-year-old physician with a twelve-year-old son, who took to Justin right away. Despite her good looks, Justin was simply not attracted to her.

As I continued my quest on Justin's behalf, he called to tell me that he had met Sheryl on his own through a dating site, which surprised me. "He must have gotten restless and decided to try his luck online after his last frustrating experience," I thought. Sure enough, he and Sheryl hit it off beautifully, so he requested that his membership be put on "hold" so that he could focus on getting to know her.

Justin and Sheryl turned out to be polar opposites politically. She was a staunch conservative Republican who had a huge social circle and chose friendships with like-minded individuals. She had never dated a liberal before but was so attracted to Justin that she decided to give it a try. They simply agreed to disagree and tried not to let their differences interfere with their budding romance.

Once they became serious, however, their differences extended to their families and friends. Sheryl's father, who was retired from the military, had raised her with conservative values and couldn't understand why she had chosen Justin; he was mistrustful of him and his motives. Justin's friends were also concerned. Knowing him as they did, they wondered how in the world he would tolerate Sheryl's views.

In my practice, I took great care to assess compatibility based on a variety of considerations, including political beliefs. It seemed as if, over the years, my clients had become less and less tolerant of differences, to the point where they became deal breakers rather than just factors to weigh in the matching process. I probably would not have matched Justin with a woman who held Sheryl's beliefs, but I was respectful of his choice and encouraged him to keep his eye on the "big picture" with Sheryl rather than getting bogged down with other people's opinions of what was best for them. This was easier said than done.

Their relationship went through serious challenges as they became more deeply enmeshed with each other's families and friends. Their first Christmas at Sheryl's parents' home turned toxic when Justin and Sheryl's father argued over politics and neither would back down despite Sheryl's pleas to get Justin to tone it down. Her parents viewed him as intransigent and tried to discourage Sheryl from continuing the relationship. Meanwhile, Justin's children had become somewhat attached to Sheryl, and she and her son had developed feelings for them as well. She was therefore reluctant to walk away, as her family advised.

There was also an imbalance in their financial situations. Justin had considerable wealth, while Sheryl lived paycheck to paycheck as a guidance counselor and single mom. Understandably, if they married, Justin was concerned about protecting his children's inheritance since he was their only living parent. Justin's friends also gave Sheryl some "bad press," thinking that she could potentially exploit him for his money. Nothing could have been further from the truth, but Justin's friends didn't know Sheryl well enough to have those assurances and feared the worst for Justin.

With my coaching and support, which I provide even while a client's account is on "hold," Justin consulted his former divorce attorney to discuss drafting a prenuptial agreement, which made sense, given his financial exposure. She drafted a comprehensive agreement that Justin thought was very fair to Sheryl and, in keeping with his lawyer's recommendation, he suggested that she seek her own legal counsel to review the document and advise her.

After much back and forth between the attorneys, they settled on an agreement they could both live with and got engaged, pledging not to let anything, be it politics, money, family, or friends, interfere in their happiness.

They have now been happily married for fifteen years and have shared in the joy of their children's weddings, and the arrival of grandchildren, as well as the tragedy of losing parents. Through it all, Justin and Sheryl have been able to withstand their differences due to the strength of their love and commitment to their marriage, the strong physical chemistry between them, and the shared values of family, which transcended their political differences. They also sought couples therapy at pivotal points in their marriage to help them navigate certain challenges they encountered along the way. They are a sterling example of a couple succeeding against most odds and a testament to the emotional maturity that it takes to embrace the things that connected them, rather than dwelling on their differences.

## CHAPTER TWENTY-NINE

# The Goldilocks Marriage

*A*bout a year into our relationship, Jim began surfing the real estate sites online to see what was on the market in our area. This was a very good sign. We had talked about getting a new place together, and while nothing official had happened yet, this research felt reassuring and exciting. He would show me various homes, and we would talk about what we liked, could afford, etc. One property that we had admired had been on and off the market in nearby Garrett Park. It was now back on the market at a reduced price.

Garrett Park was an unusual community, tucked away between Rockville and Kensington, with only three hundred homes. It was its own municipality, had its own zip code and post office where all mail was delivered, and was situated on a MARC commuter stop with a quaint, high-end restaurant across from the train tracks. I had lived in an adjacent community when I first separated from Howard and had walked through Garrett Park on my hikes many times, admiring the old Victorian homes and the amazing horticulture. I had also eaten at the restaurant many times.

The house that Jim showed me on Zillow looked interesting. It was a contemporary design, which was unusual for Garrett Park. The split-foyer home had been completely renovated five years earlier and had some very unusual features. We e-mailed the listing agent and looked forward to learning more about the house. When we hadn't received a response by the following Sunday, I suggested that we drive over and look at it ourselves, even though it wasn't officially open that day. Jim agreed.

As we drove into Garrett Park that April morning, we were struck by the beauty of the area, with its majestic hundred-year-old trees, blooming azaleas, and elegant homes, each one unique, unlike most developments in our area. We pulled up to the house and were relieved not to see any cars in the driveway, which I presumed meant that no one was home. I got out and began peering through the floor-to-ceiling windows of the room off the driveway. Jim stood behind me, tentative and disapproving of my boldness. Suddenly, the front door opened, and a handsome man in his thirties curtly said, "Can I help you?" I was surprised and embarrassed but explained that we had been interested in the house and had e-mailed the agent but hadn't heard back.

When he realized that we were serious potential buyers, his demeanor completely changed. He warmly greeted us and invited us to come in, explaining that his family had left for the day and he'd be happy to show us around. He explained that he had purchased the property five years earlier and had renovated it from top to bottom himself.

As he showed us around, we were blown away by the quality of his work. He had taken a very ordinary split-level brick home and turned it into a contemporary showcase befitting a *Dwell Magazine* house. He had accomplished this by tearing down walls, adding baseboard paneling, putting in floor-to-ceiling windows and skylights, and replacing the doors with eight-foot oak doors. He had also cleverly installed mirrored doors on all the sliding closets to give the illusion of more space.

While the interior was decorated very sparsely, Jim and I both envisioned the possibilities. We both love decorating and have very similar taste. The layout upstairs was a bit odd for a family, however. There was a powder room, one very large bedroom, which was formerly two smaller rooms, and another smaller bedroom with a full bath. The smaller bedroom was too small to serve as a master. Because my children were already living on their own, this was a nonissue for us, but despite all the aesthetics, we were still not convinced that this was the right house for us. As we descended downstairs, however, we were sold. The owner led us through what had been a former garage, which he had transformed into a huge office with Brazilian hardwood floors. There was a bedroom to the left with a marble tile fireplace, walk-in closet, and an enormous master bath.

Jim and I were both besotted by the beauty and charm of the place. We thanked our host for the tour and departed down the driveway, at which point Jim exclaimed, "As God is my witness, this house will be mine!" Of course, I would have preferred to have heard him say "ours" instead, but I understood that this was an "excited utterance" (an applicable legal term) on his part and decided not to take it personally.

Back in the car, we eagerly discussed how we could work out the finances and decided to call Jim's former Realtor to assist us in buying the house, the only property we had ever looked at. That evening we were in her office writing up an offer. By the time we had finished, we were exhausted and famished and popped into the Oyster Grill Company, the only restaurant still open in Cabin John Shopping Center at that hour.

The restaurant was almost empty as the waitress took our order. We held hands, trying to take in the day's events. When we woke up that morning, we'd had no idea we'd be buying a house that day. Here we were, having submitted an offer that evening. Then, out of a back room in the restaurant, a group of people exited. We immediately looked up to see Deborah and Spence, our friends who had introduced us. We hadn't seen them in about six months and were shocked that, of all people, they happened to show up on this very auspicious day. This seemed like fate. We eagerly shared our news and showed them pictures of the home we hoped would be ours. Deborah said that she was sure we would get the house. We could only pray. Yet by Tuesday, our offer had been accepted, and we were well on our way to making our dream house a reality.

We had planned a trip to New York that weekend to celebrate my birthday with my sister, Evie, and her husband, Joe. Jim and I talked about how awkward it would feel to us to announce to our family that we were buying a house with no mention of marriage, even at our "advanced ages." It seemed like the right time to make it official. He asked me to meet him at Capital One Bank that Friday afternoon before we were to leave for the weekend. In the past, when we had discussed marriage in hypothetical terms, he had told me that he had a ring that had belonged to his late mother in his safety deposit box. He had said that when the time came, it could serve as an engagement ring, or, if I chose, I could have a traditional diamond solitaire instead.

That Friday afternoon, I eagerly met him at the bank. Jim completed his paperwork and lovingly ushered me into the tiny room with a table and chairs designed for customers to open their safety deposit boxes. He opened his box and removed a jewelry box, which contained a stunning antique diamond ring, offset by tiny sapphires, which had been stored there since Jim's mother's untimely death over fifty years earlier. It had been designed for her by her parents when she had been in her twenties and had not been worn at all since her passing. I loved it from the moment I saw it and had no desire to wear anything else. Jim then got down on one knee and, in that tiny room, which probably had the whole episode memorialized on security footage, proposed marriage in his unique way.

Although I knew the proposal was coming, I was still choked up with emotion as he explained his reasons for asking me to marry him. He said that besides my wonderful attributes of beauty, brains, and personality, which were a given, he was asking me to marry him because, above all else, he trusted me. He trusted that I would always honor the sacred nature of our love, which to him meant that he could always count on me in every way. That meant everything to me. As usual, he captured that sentiment brilliantly. I tearfully accepted, and we hugged and kissed in the sterile room, which to me, felt like the most romantic setting on the planet.

We set a wedding date of October 12 for the following fall, which was only six months away. Somehow, in that time, with the help of some dear friends and family members, we managed to buy and move into our new home, sell and empty out my condo and Jim's house, and plan a wedding. The sequence of our relationship had been unconventional. We had started with the honeymoon, bought a house, got engaged, moved in, and then married. From the start, we had forged our own path, which felt totally right for us.

We chose a wedding venue in DC. The Mansion on O Street in Dupont Circle was a magical place, which consisted of adjoining townhouses connected internally that served as a party venue, bed and breakfast, and rock 'n' roll museum. Each room was lovingly decorated with a particular theme and filled with art, photographs, figurines, and rock-'n'-roll memorabilia, all available for sale.

I had been introduced to that venue years earlier when my daughter had attended her graduation party from the Charles E. Smith Jewish Day School there. She had been a classmate of the owners' son, and they had generously hosted their graduating class there. It had the perfect combination of elegance and tasteful excess, with fascinating objects filling every space in every room as far as the eye could see. Guests were invited to sip champagne as they toured the many guest rooms on all three levels. Jim had not known of the place, but, as I anticipated, he was enchanted by it as a former rock-'n'-roll musician. When we discussed what kind of wedding we wanted, I suggested the Mansion on O Street, and Jim was instantly onboard with the idea. This would be no ordinary wedding, reflecting the fact that we were far from an ordinary couple.

On October 12, 2013, we were married. Jim and I arranged for our stay at the Mansion on O Street, along with our wedding party, to make the experience even more special. A weekend of celebration ensued with about eighty guests in attendance, including friends and family from as far away as Israel, London, and California.

Jim agreed to a Jewish ceremony, and we were blessed to have my dear friend Rabbi Tamara Miller officiate, which lent a personal intimacy to the traditional ceremony. My beloved ninety-year-old uncle Benno from London, who was a surrogate father to me, walked me down the aisle. We also honored our friends who had introduced us by asking them, along with my cousins who had traveled from London, to hold up the sides of our *chuppah* (wedding canopy).

After the ceremony, we partied until the wee hours of the night. Jim had arranged the music, a wedding mix, which we started with a *horah*, effected in the usual Jewish tradition of raising both bride and groom up on chairs as guests danced around them. While Jim was a good sport about it, he was totally terrified when he was lifted up, which we memorialized in the perfect photo that makes us laugh hysterically every time we look at our wedding album.

We continued the festivities with all of our favorite dance tunes. As a gift to our guests, we gave them copies of the mix tape Jim had made for me when we first fell in love. He designed the CD case with photos of us from Santorini and the California coast, which we drove down together a year after our trip to Greece. Our wedding was my dream come true: the Goldilocks wedding, my third and, finally, the perfect wedding I had longed for my entire life. It was almost exactly a year and half since Jim and I had first met. Now the real work of being *in* the marriage was about to begin.

## CHAPTER THIRTY

# Leave Your Baggage Behind

$\mathcal{G}$etting beyond one's baggage always depends on the particular issues one is trying to move forward from. Obviously, therapy is one important and effective tool because it brings in a trained, neutral third party to evaluate one's history and process the reasons for falling into particular patterns. In my practice, I've witnessed many problems that could have been avoided had therapy been incorporated into the divorce process.

Edie was a shapely, vivacious blonde woman in her late fifties who had lost her husband, Ken, three years prior to meeting with me. During her consultation, she tearfully explained that she had lived a wonderful life with her late husband, a physician, to whom she'd been married for thirty years and who had been a fantastic husband, father, and provider. He had been the primary bread winner, although Edie had worked herself as a guidance counselor once their two children became of school age. They lived in a large, beautifully decorated home in Potomac, Maryland, on a property befitting a successful cardiologist. Edie was the proud mother of two grown sons; one was a physician, the other an attorney. They were both happily married and had three children between them.

Edie's marriage had been a fairly traditional one, with Ken being in charge of their finances and Edie doing most of the childrearing. She was accustomed to having her financial and material needs taken care of while she attended to the business of running the family. Losing Ken was particularly crushing for her for many reasons, not the least of which was financial. Although she was fortunate that he had left her ample resources to live out the rest of her life comfortably, she was now left to organize her own finances, which felt very overwhelming to her.

After mourning Ken for three years, Edie decided that she was ready to get back into the dating world. She hoped to meet a good man through my service rather than subjecting herself to the stress of online dating. After spending a few hours with Edie, I decided to introduce her to Mel, a smart, cute, and funny divorced man in his midsixties. Mel was a tall, solidly built man who exuded intelligence and charm. He had curly salt-and-pepper hair, striking blue eyes, and an easy smile. An attorney colleague of mine had introduced Mel to me as someone who would be a good addition to my database. He wasn't interested in hiring me, which he had explained over coffee together, but would be happy to meet anyone whom I was actively working with if I thought they'd be a good match.

Mel had been through a difficult divorce. He had felt financially exploited by his ex-wife, who had gotten their house, along with substantial alimony and child support in their divorce settlement. Mel was very resentful of this outcome and, as a result, extremely sensitive to the issue of being taken advantage of by any woman he dated. He was only interested in an "egalitarian relationship," as he put it, and was seeking a partner with a similar philosophy in every way, including financial.

My instincts told me that Edie and Mel would be attracted to each other. I was right. Edie was surprised and thrilled to have met someone exciting to her right out of the "starting gate" after her years of celibacy. Mel was smitten and launched a romantic campaign that few women could resist. He chose romantic restaurants and took her dancing, to concerts, to the theater, and on day trips all over the area, from the mountains to the west, to the beaches to the east. They were having a blast.

Edie phoned me with an update about two months into their newly blossoming relationship. She excitedly told me that she was getting ready to become intimate with Mel and had gone on a shopping spree at Victoria's Secret for a new lingerie collection in anticipation of this auspicious event. "There's just one thing that bothers me," she confided. "Whenever we've been out together and the check comes, Mel always suggests that we split it. I've agreed since I haven't wanted to make an issue of it then and there, but I really haven't liked it. It feels very awkward to me to be opening my wallet at the table. Remember, I was in a marriage where my husband paid for everything, so it's uncomfortable for me to pay my own way when we're out. Mind you, I'm happy to share in my own way, by cooking dinners or buying theater tickets. It's not like I expect him to foot the bill for everything. I just don't like being asked to pay when we're out. Does that make sense?"

"Of course it does," I responded. "Mel is a very different kind of man than Ken was, and you're not used to his kind of sharing. I get it. Perhaps if I explain this to Mel," I offered, "he might soften up in this regard."

"Feel free," she suggested. "It might be better coming from you than from me."

"I'll give it my best shot," I told her.

"Mel, I'm delighted to hear things are going so well between you and Edie," I began. "Edie has told me how much fun you're having, and I couldn't be happier for you two," I said. "There's just one issue that concerns her," I continued. "She's a fairly traditional woman and therefore feels uncomfortable splitting a check in a restaurant. She'd much prefer to contribute in her own way rather than splitting a check every time you go out. It's just not what she's used to. She's hoping you'll understand," I cautiously ventured.

"Leora, this is absolutely nonnegotiable," he responded. "I've been taken advantage of in the past and swore never to put myself in that position again."

"But Edie isn't looking to do that," I said, trying to reason with him. "She's very comfortable financially and certainly isn't looking for anyone else to support her. She just wants to 'feel like a lady' when she's taken out. She enjoys having a man occupy a more traditional role in public, but that doesn't mean she's not willing to do her fair share." As I tried to reason further with Mel, I could feel him becoming more strident in his position. "Mel, I'm not trying to put you on the defensive at all. Just think about how rare and special your connection to Edie has been. All I'm suggesting are some stylistic changes so you can *both* feel comfortable in the relationship," I reasoned.

Mel wasn't having it. I asked him whether this issue was worth sacrificing the relationship for, and, to my surprise and regret, he insisted it was. It seemed to me that it wasn't even about Edie as much as it was about Mel defending his position. I felt very sad for him. The wound from his divorce had run very deep. Any semblance of someone wanting something from him was apparently intolerable.

I went back to Edie and explained that he was unwilling to budge on this issue, for reasons that were understandable, based on his history. I asked her whether she might be able to work with him on this, at least until the relationship got further along, but she was sadly unwilling herself.

I couldn't believe that they were both prepared to throw away their good fortune in finding one another. I asked myself whether

I had made a mistake introducing them in the first place, given their respective histories. On the other hand, my experience as a matchmaker had taught me to cherish and encourage matches where both the chemistry and the connection were present from the beginning. But I was unable to help either of them move beyond their comfort zones to cultivate a new reality, where the rules of engagement were different from what they were used to.

Betty and Richard are another example of a couple's inability to move beyond their emotional baggage. Betty was in the middle of a divorce when I introduced her to Richard, who was going through the same process himself. He was a landscape architect who managed his own business. She had shared with me that she was particularly attracted to men who were bald with facial hair. Richard fit that description to a T. He was a handsome fellow a few years younger than Betty. He'd decided to shave his head when he began to go bald and had a sporty goatee, which complemented his designer glasses. Betty, a physical therapist, was equally as stylish in her own way. She thought Richard was hip and exuded an "alpha male" sexuality, which she found very appealing.

She was in her midfifties, with curly blonde hair, big brown eyes, and a figure that most twenty-year-olds would envy. She had two sons in their twenties, who were somewhat troubled as a result of the divorce, despite the fact that Betty had worked hard to get her sons the therapy they needed to process the breakdown of their family.

Richard, the father of a preteen daughter and a son with special needs, understood and empathized with Betty's situation and was a wonderful sounding board for her as she navigated the ups and downs of her divorce. Betty, in turn, supported Richard, who was struggling with a toxic situation with his ex-wife.

They fell for each other very quickly. I was thrilled for them. Their relationship deepened into commitment within six months of dating. Eventually, after two years together, they both finalized their divorces and decided to buy a house together. Neither of them were ready to consider marriage after just becoming disentangled from their former spouses, but they were deeply in love and wanted to build a home together as the next step in their relationship.

They bought a house on a large wooded property that appealed to them both, since they shared a love of nature and animals. They also bought a border collie puppy who was lucky enough to roam the property freely and be raised in "doggy paradise."

Betty's settlement money provided the down payment to their house, and they entered into a prenuptial agreement, which stated that if they separated, Richard would pay off his share of the down payment. At the time, they both considered the agreement to be a purely academic exercise recommended by their respective lawyers, and one they simply stuck in a drawer and thought they would never need to invoke.

They cohabited happily for about a year until issues surrounding their children intervened. Betty felt that Richard was too focused on his own children to support her given the stress of her own boys, one of whom had become even more alienated from her, something that deeply depressed her. Richard felt that his hands were full with his own children's needs. His daughter was unhappy with their living situation and resented having to share her weekends with her father and his girlfriend, whom she didn't feel particularly close to or welcomed by. His son was only ten years old when they moved in together and required continued supervision. When Richard had to work some weekends and asked Betty to look after his son, she refused, resenting the request and feeling unfairly burdened by his expectations of her as a "stepparent."

Financial differences also impacted the relationship. Betty was in a strong financial position, while Richard still struggled to keep his business afloat. Betty began to resent Richard's limited resources, something that hadn't been an issue before they moved in together.

She craved adventure and dreamed of trips abroad, which Richard was unable to afford. That, along with her unwillingness to occupy a stepparent role to his children, began to erode their relationship. Betty became increasingly unhappy, which caused their sex life to dwindle as well. Eventually, they went from blissful lovers to roommates who didn't get along.

Betty decided she wanted out. Despite their best intentions, their separation was messy and a painful reminder of the trauma they had each suffered in their respective divorces. By the time they actually split up, lawyers were involved, and they ended up in court to enforce the prenup that they had hoped would remain tucked away in a drawer forever.

Had Richard and Betty worked with a skilled family therapist to negotiate their expectations before moving in together, their relationship might have been salvaged. Instead, they made some very fundamental yet faulty assumptions based on their own needs rather than on an understanding of what each of them was capable and/or willing to provide to the other. They were much further along in their relationship than Edie and Mel, but both scenarios demonstrate how critically important it is to work out one's own emotional baggage before trying to move forward in a new relationship.

Sometimes getting beyond one's baggage is simply a question of taking the time to recover from loss or trauma in a former relationship. Failure to do so may cause the next relationship to backfire. Rachel, an attractive seventy-year-old divorcee, met Harold, a tall, handsome widower about her age, at a singles' presentation. Harold had lost his wife only two months earlier and was there for the program rather than to meet women. Rachel was highly attracted to Harold and tracked him down through the organizer of the event, asking her to convey her interest to Harold. Harold was surprised and flattered to learn that he had an admirer and decided to give Rachel a call.

Rachel and Harold began dating while Harold still attended his weekly grief and loss support group. When Rachel shared this new development with me, I cautioned her to be careful not to become Harold's therapist rather than his love interest. As time went on, it became clear to Rachel that Harold was not over his loss. He would never have her over to his home, would not socialize with her with any of his couple friends, and would not introduce her to his children, even after a year had passed since his wife's death. Eventually, Harold admitted to Rachel that while he adored his time with her, he wasn't "in love" and therefore thought it best for both of them to move on. Rachel was devastated.

While it's impossible to know what would have happened had they not met so soon after the loss of Harold's wife, the probabilities were not in Rachel's favor from the beginning. Harold was more than happy to have Rachel in his life, but what he needed wasn't a distraction. He needed time to process and grieve his loss, without the pressure of a new relationship.

Whether moving forward requires putting one's house in order, taking the time needed to mourn, or get therapy will depend on the nature of each person's issues. We alone are responsible for handling them. Expecting a new partner to magically clear all that up is unrealistic and sets the new partner up for failure, an outcome that is entirely avoidable by acting responsibly after the loss of a relationship, whatever the circumstances.

## CHAPTER THIRTY-ONE

# *Let the Real Work Begin*

My personal story exemplifies the benefits of therapy. After my separation from Howard, I fell into the usual pattern of blaming him for our problems rather than looking inward to figure out what I had contributed to the demise of the marriage as well. The easiest thing is to assign blame and to carry around resentment like a warm, comfortable cloak as justification for how the other party has wronged us. It's much harder to take responsibility for our own piece of the dysfunction and to figure out how to avoid making similar mistakes in the future. In my case, with the help of a skilled therapist, whom I saw weekly during my separation, I came to understand the reasons why I had entered into my marriage to Howard in the first place.

The old adage that women look for their fathers and men their mothers in a mate certainly applied in my case. I had been raised by a strong, loving, yet controlling mother and a sweet, mostly passive father who was content to let my mother call the shots. He believed this to be a healthy model based on the power dynamic he had experienced in his own household growing up in a small town in Poland. The fact that he had picked my mother, a capable go-getter, as his partner came as no surprise.

When I married Howard, my father gave me a few words of advice: "Men don't really know what's going on in life. *You* be the one to push your husband." I took this to mean that while Howard had a plan for his profession, it would be my job to figure out where and how to live, how to furnish our home, when to have children, and, once the children arrived, how we would educate and raise them. I presumed that, like my father, Howard would simply go along with whatever I wanted. His sweetness and deference to me during our courtship had led to that assumption.

Once in the marriage, however, I learned that Howard was not my father and he had his own childhood baggage that he struggled with. My expectation that the major choices in our lives were mine alone to make was not only unrealistic but also completely unfair to him. With my therapist's help, I figured out that another common thread between Howard and my father was an undercurrent of resentment that they both carried. They weren't truly happy to find themselves in the passive role, even if they complied with their wives' wishes. Howard manifested his resistance to me by taking a position and not budging, despite my pleas that he see things my way. I was quite shocked by this aspect of his personality, which hadn't revealed itself before we got married. After all, this wasn't my father, who grudgingly complied, but a completely different person with his own history and emotional triggers.

I didn't like not getting my way. In the course of my therapy, I came to understand that I gradually became more and more like my mother in that relationship, hoping I would eventually wear him down the longer I pleaded with him. When that didn't happen, my own anger got activated and carved away at our marriage until there was nothing left but anger on both sides. This realization has prevented me from picking a similar partner, and while I didn't find the right formula in a partner for several more relationships, I didn't repeat *that* particular pattern.

Marrying Jim thirty years later was a much healthier decision and a reflection of the psychological progress I had made in my relationships. Nevertheless, issues and challenges unique to Jim and me inevitably presented themselves, and, like many couples, when conflicts arose in our marriage, we were thrown off balance and struggled to handle them effectively.

While I had eagerly awaited my departure from my job as an attorney so that I could focus exclusively on my business, as an extrovert, I had enjoyed working among colleagues and friends on a daily basis. Once I left my government position in 2015 and began working from home, it was a new, challenging reality. I lacked a support system and had to be entirely self-driven. While I had taken almost a year to develop a business plan and put money aside to implement it, I found it stressful to make all the decisions on my own. I was wise enough to consult a handful of professionals to support my goals, but I was mindful of costs and struggled with the tough decisions inherent in running a business on my own.

For the first time, Jim and I had very different stressors. He continued to work at his job but unexpectedly began to experience health problems, including migraine headaches in the two years leading up to his retirement. I was building my home-based business, where I was faced with the typical household problems like appliances breaking down as well as structural problems, which came as a surprise to us both.

Jim had been accustomed to maintaining his previous home without input from his late wife, who was happy to let him handle those issues. I, however, had to deal with the issues when they came up, since I was home every day and Jim wasn't. This led to an unforeseen power struggle between us. I was determined to understand and cope with those issues for fear of becoming dependent upon Jim. Jim felt frustrated by my efforts, feeling as if I were undermining his expertise. This was a formula for trouble.

To make matters even more challenging, our styles are very different, and when we disagreed, we rubbed each other the wrong way. Mine was a "take charge" style, and Jim's was one of quiet control. We both wanted to be "captain of the ship" and had little patience for the other's attempts to help or intervene. After a series of arguments that left us both feeling unappreciated and wounded, I suggested that we get some couples counseling to work on that part of our relationship. I was determined to do it right this time. Much to my relief, as a psychologist who'd done a significant amount of therapy himself, Jim was open to the idea.

We decided to find a neutral therapist whom neither of us had worked with previously and who specialized in Imago therapy, a technique pioneered by Dr. Harville Hendrix. I had learned about it from my friend Deborah, who had introduced me to Jim and had been trained in this discipline, which she successfully employed in her practice with couples. Imago therapy teaches that one's love interest embodies both the positive and negative qualities of both parents, which offers another explanation for why chemistry exists between particular people. Couples are schooled in communication techniques such as mirroring, which teaches a dialogue technique designed to provide each party with a deeper understanding and empathy for the other's position before trying to come up with solutions. I had read *Getting the Love You Want* years earlier, and this approach resonated with me.

We learned about Sandra from my friend Cindy. Sandra had been working with Cindy as an individual therapist for years. Cindy and I had hit a rough patch in our friendship, and she requested that I participate in a session with her therapist. While I apprehensively agreed, I ended up being highly impressed with Sandra after she not only successfully resolved the issue between Cindy and me but also managed to get to the root of the problem.

When Jim and I thought about whom we might work with, I suggested we call Sandra. Jim agreed, and Sandra scheduled a time to meet with us.

In our initial session in which we aired our grievances, Sandra reframed the conversation so that each of us were directed to acknowledge each other's strengths as well as the other's position. We followed her prompts, step-by-step, and engaged in the mirroring technique I had previously read about. It was amazing how quickly our anger dissipated once we each felt heard and acknowledged by the other. It almost made whatever issue we were addressing feel insignificant. We each learned what drove our positions. Jim realized that because he had lost his mother when he was only ten years old and had subsequently been raised by a father who was largely a hands-off parent, Jim had developed a sense of competency by handling problems on his own. When I challenged that competency, it was a natural trigger for anger on his part. I, on the other hand, had been raised by a very loving but controlling mother who had inadvertently fostered dependency that terrified me as an adult. That was my trigger. Our new marriage had brought up my fear about being dependent upon my husband.

The communication skills we learned, as well as many other insights, helped us to become more sensitive to each other's triggers. We also learned to ask for help in new and different ways that did not threaten each other's self-esteem and allowed us to support each other more effectively. We looked forward to our sessions and found ourselves much more tuned in to each other as a result of doing this work together. After about ten sessions with Sandra, Jim and I felt that we had mastered the mirroring techniques and could incorporate them into our relationship on our own. Sandra was gratified by the results she witnessed with us and offered her ongoing support in the future.

I found myself encouraged and energized by the couples work we did. I was also thrilled to have finally found a partner who had the courage to look inward, the intellect to process the work, and the motivation to make our marriage succeed. "This must be the 'healing' that the books talk about," I thought. It felt wonderful to be accepted for who I was, "warts" and all, and to be truly loved in spite of them.

One year after we completed our couple's work, Jim retired from his government position and began his private practice. We were then faced with the new adjustment of us both working from home during the day. Our rhythms and schedules were different, and I had to make sure to stay on task without being distracted by Jim's presence or to succumb to the temptation to "play" when there was work to be done. Jim's discipline and ability to focus has helped to ensure that we have both continued to be productive.

Our demanding schedules, which still involve working many evenings and weekends, have made us appreciate our leisure time together even more. There have been many ups and downs as we've learned to navigate this territory. Yet it continues to be a journey that, from my perspective, has been a resounding success.

## Chapter Thirty-Two

# Success with Benefits

*M*y matchmaking career has been especially gratifying when the couples I've introduced have produced children. These successful outcomes have gone a long way toward balancing the referrals that didn't succeed, despite all the finessing I might have employed to promote the "match." As in most relationships, whether business, platonic, or romantic, the issue usually boils down to whether the right chemistry exists, in whatever capacity the parties are connected.

Mindy and Sam are perfect examples of this. Mindy, was a thirty-nine-year-old lawyer who had moved to the DC area from Chicago to join a prestigious law firm after clerking for a federal judge. She had pursued law as a second career after working in the accounting field since receiving her CPA.

Calling her goal oriented would be putting it mildly. She had a stellar career and was now ready to put that same drive into her personal life by meeting the right man and starting a family. She was attractive, not beautiful, but what made her especially desirable was her sparkling intelligence, warmth, and sense of humor.

She sat in my office describing her family dynamics, which were more or less healthy and stable, and her past relationships, which had all been with high-functioning, emotionally available men. I was excited to be working with her, since her history boded well for future success. She was emotionally available and ready to pursue this new stage in her life. She just needed help in accessing the kind of man who would be appropriate for her.

Sam was a forty-five-year-old lobbyist who'd never been married, but adored children. The eldest of four children, he had grown up in a stable family on Long Island. His standards were high, thus he hadn't found the woman he wanted to marry, although he'd had very loving relationships and stayed friends with all of his former girlfriends. This most recent girlfriend, Jen, whom he'd dated for two years, was a few years older than him and a single mom of three children.

It had been a very healing relationship for Jen, having come out of a nasty divorce when her children were between five and eleven years old. Sam had not only provided a safe haven for Jen but had also bonded with her children, providing them with a male presence in their lives. After being such an important part of Jen's family, Sam realized how much he wanted to start his own family. Jen was grateful to have had his support during a difficult transition in her life and understood and respected Sam's need to move on, so much so that she referred Sam to me.

I was impressed with Sam from the start. He was a tall, handsome, and energetic fellow. Goodness seemed to naturally flow out of him, and I was delighted to welcome him into my network. I decided to introduce him to Mindy since their ages, goals, values, and levels of accomplishment all seemed to match up. Sam liked Mindy right away, but Mindy was hesitant about the chemistry between them.

"I can see that Sam is a special man," she told me after they'd been out a few times. "And I can definitely see why you introduced us. I just don't feel any romantic spark for him," she lamented.

"I understand," I responded. "We both agree that men like Sam don't come along every day. If I were you," I advised, "I'd keep spending time with him. At a minimum, you'll enjoy a nice friendship, and maybe you'll start to feel differently over time. In my experience, chemistry doesn't always happen right away. Give it a chance."

> *In my experience, chemistry doesn't always happen right away.*

She agreed. Of course, I knew that Sam was attracted to her and would not have advised her to hang in there unless I was confident that Sam would be patient and welcome the opportunity to get involved with her when she was ready.

Three months later, Mindy called to report that she and Sam had "become inseparable." I was thrilled to hear it. "How did that come about?" I asked.

"Well, I took your advice and just got together with him as friends for a while. I became more and more impressed by him over time. Meanwhile, I had been feeling like I wanted to lose some weight. So I went on a diet and lost ten pounds. Suddenly, he started looking more appealing to me!"

"How interesting," I thought. It seems that the holdup wasn't any lack of attractiveness on Sam's part but Mindy's feelings about herself. Once she felt more desirable, she began to feel receptive to an intimate relationship with Sam, and it blossomed from there. After dating for about a year, Mindy and Sam got engaged and married a year later. They have two sons and live in Potomac, Maryland.

Their success would not have been possible without wisdom and patience on both their parts. Sam was smart enough to identify that Mindy was worth waiting for. Mindy was smart enough to take my advice and give it time. She also worked on her own issues during this time, wanting to be her "best self" and at a weight she felt happy with. Had she not made the effort to do so, she might not have been as open to Sam physically, and eventually, he might have lost interest. They are a wonderful example of doing whatever it takes to recognize and nurture opportunities where they exist.

Sometimes, chemistry can be the outcome of a recognition that the person has something unique to offer, aside from or in addition to their looks.

Dennis, a strikingly handsome forty-year-old, was a newcomer to the DC area. He had grown up in Oakland, California, and had moved to DC for a job in the high-tech industry. He told me that he was ready to settle down and he had no problem meeting women, but meeting the *right* woman had eluded him so far.

I thought carefully about the right match for Dennis and decided to introduce him to Rita, an occupational therapist who was pretty, but not gorgeous. With her athletic figure, long brown hair, and big brown eyes, she had a wholesome "girl next door" quality about her. I reasoned that finding him someone at his level of physical beauty might cause them to compete with each other in the looks department.

That calculation paid off. Rita called me right after the date, letting me know that she really liked Dennis, which did not surprise me in the least. Not only was he "movie-star level gorgeous," but he also had a sweetness to him, which was unusual for someone so handsome. She said that they'd had a great first date and that she hoped to see him again. I let her know that I would get back to her with my recommendation once I received feedback from Dennis.

Dennis called a day later to thank me for introducing him to Rita. He said that she was just as I had described her. She was lovely, sweet, and smart, but just "not his type." He requested a new referral.

"That's fine," I told him, "but before we move on, can you tell me more about your date with Rita?"

"Sure," he said. "Well, we spent the day walking the Cabin John Trail from Bethesda into Georgetown and grabbed a bite to eat once we got to Georgetown."

"Sounds great," I said. " Exactly how long were you together?"

"About eight hours," he responded.

"Eight hours?" I replied. "That's an unusually long time to spend together on a first date," I remarked. "You must have had a lot to say to each other for all that time."

"Well, actually, yes," he continued. "She's very low-key, which made me very comfortable, and the conversation flowed really easily. We discovered that we had much more in common than we originally thought. Plus, she has a great sense of humor, and we laughed a lot through a rather challenging walk. She's in great shape as well and managed to keep up the pace for the entire six-mile hike."

"Dennis," I responded, "I must tell you that this is a very unusual first-date experience. Most people meet initially for a few hours, no more, and then decide if a second date makes sense. You guys seemed to have had about three first dates in one, with all the time you spent together. The fact that you had so much to say to each other, without the usual awkwardness that happens on a first date, is something to pay attention to. I wouldn't be so quick to dismiss it. You might find that spending more time together is even more satisfying. Why not give it at least another try?"

"Maybe so," he replied. "I did have a great time with her and admire a lot of her qualities. I guess I have nothing to lose by seeing her again."

I was encouraged by his willingness to give Rita another chance and reported back to her that he had a great time and would like to see her again. Of course, I did not share his doubts with

her, since my conversation with Dennis was confidential, and I
didn't want to raise any concerns on her part. I wanted Rita to
go into their second date with confidence and optimism. They
went out again and again, as it turned out. Dennis became more
attracted and attached to her as time went on, despite the fact
that he was not accustomed to dating a less glamorous woman.
Rita encouraged Dennis in his new position, showed him around
town, and gave him the confidence to pursue his career goals and,
ultimately, her. They married and had two gorgeous daughters,
their beauty coming as no surprise.

There has been a special joy in knowing that children came
into this world as a result of my efforts. Yet my objective
has always been to find love for my clients, whether or not it
produced children. In fact, one of my successful matches was a
couple who decided not to have children together. Beth was a
thirty-one-year-old woman who had overcome a life-threatening
illness in her twenties, which made her much more mature for
her age than her contemporaries. She had been raised in the
DC area but was living in Miami, where she was attending the
university to complete undergraduate work from which she had
taken a break during her illness and recovery. Her parents, who
lived in the DC area, hired me to find her a match, whether in
the DC area or in Florida.

Despite my best efforts at recruiting for her in the Miami area, I
ended up finding a man for her in Northern Virginia. Beth visited
her family often enough that she was open to what amounted to a
long-distance relationship, especially since her ultimate goal was
to return to the DC area. She was a very attractive, tall, slightly
overweight redhead who was self-conscious about her weight and
therefore wanted to meet someone who wasn't going to "fat-shame"
her, as she put it.

I introduced her to Andy, the son of a woman I knew in
the community. Andy was thirty-six and had broken off an

engagement about a year earlier and was ready to move on. Andy lived in a very large luxury townhouse that he'd shared with his former fiancée. It was largely vacant, except for the gym he'd installed in the basement, which Beth found somewhat intimidating. Andy was a large, stocky fellow himself. He had recently lost thirty pounds and was working hard to keep it off. Despite the fact that Beth didn't have the "perfect" figure, Andy was interested in dating her. Beth, however, couldn't help being plagued by doubts, given his obsession with fitness.

They dated over a three-month period, meeting when Beth would come up to visit her family. She liked Andy but was having trouble reading his signals. Despite my efforts to reach out to Andy, he refused to share his feedback with me, which was not only frustrating but also a violation of my protocol as a matchmaker. I was therefore unable to provide any intervention, which is usually an integral part of my service.

After Beth's last date with Andy, she called to tell me it was over. She told me that she'd spent that Sunday hanging out with him. They'd gone to brunch and had had a few drinks, after which he suggested they go back to his place and rest. They'd napped in his bed, and when they woke up, Beth had expected him to finally make his move. Much to her shock and disappointment, however, he sat up and told her that he "didn't feel attracted to her" and that he thought she should leave.

To her credit, she did not allow herself to be dismissed so abruptly. She deftly engaged him in a meaningful conversation about what was happening between them. She told him that if she left, per his request, it would be the last time he'd see her. When faced with this ultimatum, he softened and said that he didn't mean that she should leave forever but that he was just feeling too much pressure from her at that time. She bravely told him that she felt very attracted to him and she thought he should be more open to a physical relationship with her, which took him aback.

He wasn't used to being with a woman who spoke her mind. He wasn't sure how to respond, so they decided to simply table the "us" conversation and have dinner together.

Beth told me that after that interaction, she didn't hold out much hope that things would turn around but felt much better about herself for standing up to him and for being honest with him. It was unfortunate that he didn't have Beth's skills or courage. We both decided that she was better off without him and that it would be best for her to move on.

Beth decided to move back to the DC area. After she got settled in a new condo in the District, I suggested that we meet and discuss how best to move forward. At that meeting, she told me that she'd been doing a lot of soul searching recently and decided she no longer wanted children of her own. She said that she was tired of meeting men close to her own age who were interested in starting families, since it felt like too much pressure on her. She no longer wanted the responsibility of being a mom. She could see herself with an older man, she said, and told me that I should not be concerned with an age difference and simply focus on finding her a good man. She also decided to apply to graduate school for a degree in social work rather than business, which was her former career path. Clearly, she had reconfigured her entire future.

My mind immediately went to Jason, who was in his midfifties and divorced with two children in their twenties. Jason was a psychotherapist with a practice in Bethesda. He was a cute, somewhat chunky but active fellow with dark, curly hair, glasses, and a beard. He had been single for several years since his divorce and had tried to meet women through friends and family, as well as online, without success. I knew he had a very big heart and was a great dad but didn't want any more children.

I showed Beth his photo, and she said that she thought he was cute and I had her permission to contact Jason on her behalf to see if he was interested. I then called Jason to ask whether he'd be open to meeting a much younger woman and explained Beth's circumstances. Not surprisingly, the idea of a younger woman appealed to him. I e-mailed him her photo, and he responded enthusiastically. He was excited that she wanted to go into a similar profession as his and said that if things worked out, he could serve as a mentor to her in the application process to graduate school and in the profession in general.

Beth's report after their first date was extremely positive. She agreed that Jason was a really nice guy who seemed to like her very much. She sensed he was immediately attracted to her, which led her to open up more readily to him. They shared a significant amount of very personal information with each other, achieving a depth in their conversation that they both recognized as highly unusual for a first date. Beth's only concern was that Jason seemed to be ready to be in a relationship with her after only one date, which made her nervous.

I understood Beth's apprehension. She wanted to make sure that he was interested in *her*, not just her qualifications as a potential girlfriend. I told her that she was absolutely right to pay attention to that. I myself had encountered the kind of man in my dating life who wanted to "close the deal" right away without having a real understanding of who I actually was.

I advised her that it was within her power to set the pace of the relationship and no matter how enthusiastic Jason might be, it was totally her call as to whether to go further with him. Knowing her sexual history, I also advised her not to become intimate with him for at least ten dates, or several months, whichever was longer. She was surprised to hear me say that. I explained that my advice wasn't due to being judgmental about sex in the early stages of dating. Rather, it was a result of my observations and experience in matching clients, as well as my own dating experience. It seemed as if men valued and saw greater romantic potential with a woman who took her time when it came to intimacy. It gave them both a chance to build a more stable foundation of friendship, which increased the likelihood that love, rather than lust, would be the driving force in their relationship. Given what Beth had been through with Andy, as well as with previous men, I wanted to help her build a healthy long-term connection rather than settling for short-term gratification.

Jason's feedback was equally as positive. He said he could absolutely see long-term potential, even after only one date. She was extremely smart, he observed, and open to feedback. Plus, her story regarding her health scare in the past had touched him deeply. He respected her courage and determination to move forward in her life professionally as well and wanted to do everything he could to support her in her goals.

"That's wonderful," I told him. "Let's just take it one step at a time."

Only two months later, Beth sent me a text saying, "Leora, Jason is an incredible guy. You may have accomplished something significant with this one. I can't believe it, to be honest."

I was thrilled. One month later, she sent a follow-up text, as millennials are prone to do. "BTW, we are in love. He is taking me to meet his mother." This was the ultimate leap of faith for a Jewish man.

# AFTERWORD

*M*y practice continues to stimulate, frustrate, educate, and inspire me on a daily basis. Just when I feel like I've heard it all, some new situation arises that surprises or confounds me. It is an ongoing testament to the complexity of human beings and relationships. I am learning more every day about myself and my clients as I try to create and foster happy and healthy connections.

I continue to collaborate with other professionals in the field. One of my trusted colleagues runs a service that assists clients with online dating. Her expertise lies in ensuring that her clients present themselves as effectively as possible; she offers an array of services that includes writing her clients' profiles and managing their online dating activity. She also makes sure that they put their best face forward, so to speak. To ensure this, she takes photos herself if she thinks a client's pictures need improvement.

During a recent dinner meeting, I asked her whether she might have anyone for a new client of mine, a divorced Jewish woman named Ellen who was in her early sixties. Ellen was looking for a successful, professional Jewish man close to her age who shared her liberal politics. She excitedly told me that she had just enrolled two new Jewish men into that age group, either of whom might work for Ellen.

"Let's take them one at a time," I told her.

"Okay," she said. "Let's start with Henry. He's sixty-four, has his own consulting company, and lives in Springfield, Virginia."

"Unfortunately, that won't work," I told her. "Ellen works downtown, lives in Columbia, and has a puppy she has to walk every evening after work. The logistics just wouldn't work between them. Can you tell me about bachelor number two?" I joked.

"Sure," she said. "Actually, I have to tell you, I think I performed a miracle with his photo. He had been using a photo that didn't do him justice at all. His clothes were all wrong, and the angle of the photo as well as the background were distracting. I advised him to buy all new clothes and sent him links to several clothing websites with specific styles I thought would flatter him. He took my advice. Here, take a look."

She turned her laptop around so that I could see both his "before" and "after" shots. My face turned crimson and must have registered shock.

"What's wrong?" she asked.

After taking a second to gather myself, I exclaimed, "That's my ex-husband, Howard!"

She was stunned. We both broke into hysterical laughter.

"Your ex? Never in a million years would I have *ever* put you two together!"

"I know," I said. "We're so different. Most people who've met the two of us, mainly through the kids, can't believe we were ever married. That was also a very long time ago," I added, as if to justify myself to her.

When I examined the photos more closely, I was impressed. She had wisely counseled Howard to update his look with more current and flattering styles, something I had tried to do during our marriage. He was still a very good-looking man, and the finished product was amazing. She had created an image that brought out the very best in Howard's features and had captured him with the wry smile I remembered so well.

"He would actually make a great match for Ellen," I said, "but I'm not touching that with a ten foot pole! That would be highly unprofessional, not to mention embarrassing." She completely agreed, so we moved on to other clients as we continued to chuckle over this for the rest of the evening.

Jeanie, a sixty-year-old physician in Cleveland and a recent addition to my membership, had spent her entire life building her career and had never been married nor had a family. She was ready to settle down and wanted a family man who was open to marriage.

I reached out to an affiliate matchmaker in her area who recommended her client Brad, a sixty-five-year old physician and attorney. I was delighted when Jeanie reported that they'd had a really great time together on their first date and she was looking forward to seeing him again. After their second date, however, they apparently got their signals crossed.

According to his matchmaker, he had incorrectly concluded that Jeanie was no longer interested in him. He based this on the fact that she didn't seem as effusive as she had been on their last date and that when they parted, she only gave him "half a hug." Jeanie was surprised to hear this. She reported that she thought the date had gone well and despite some differences that emerged on their second date, she was still interested in seeing where things might go. I called my colleague to give her this feedback, and she promised to set Brad straight and encourage him to reach out to Jeanie for a third date. We marveled at how easy it was for clients to misinterpret one another and how important our roles as caring matchmakers were to our clients' success. The feedback we offered our clients was invaluable in keeping momentum alive. Brad has now reached out to Jeanie again for a third date. Their matchmakers are standing by.

Beth and Jason got engaged within two months of meeting each other's families. I learned of this from an e-mail that Jason sent after New Year's weekend with the subject line "You did it!" I was thrilled, yet somewhat nervous to receive this news, since they had only been dating for two months before getting engaged. I had counseled Beth to wait for at least two months before becoming intimate with Jason so that they could develop a deeper foundation of emotional safety before becoming physically involved. "She must not have taken that advice," I thought, since they had gotten engaged after only two months together. "Who am I to dictate to them anyway," I thought and put my apprehensions aside to heartily congratulate them.

When I spoke to Beth shortly after to get the details, she told me that they both knew "this was it" on their first date. "I'm glad I went through everything I did in the past," she told me. "Meeting Jason made me realize that I was constantly 'trying to put a round peg in a square hole' in my relationships with men. As much as I tried, they were never right. With Jason, everything is just easy and flows. That's how I know it's right."

Other couples who married and started families through my practice seemed to have relationships that would stand the test of time, but, sadly, they didn't always work out in the end. A few years ago, I was invited to attend a singles' mixer in Virginia to help promote my business. To my surprise, Rita, whom I recognized from fifteen years earlier, came up to me and said hello. I was immediately taken aback, since I had matched her with Dennis all those years ago and knew that they had gotten married. I had heard through mutual acquaintances that they had had two children. Obviously, since she was there, they were no longer together. She explained that she was now single after divorcing Dennis two years earlier. I was saddened to hear it and asked her if she was comfortable talking about it.

"No problem," she said. "Dennis came out of the closet after we had the kids. It was hard, but I had to accept it and move on.

We're still good friends though and are doing a good job of raising our kids together."

I was amazed at Rita's compassion and graciousness. "What did I miss?" I asked myself. "Should I somehow have known this and spared Rita this trauma?"

"I'm so sorry to hear this. I hope you don't have any hard feelings toward me," I ventured.

"Not at all, Leora. You couldn't have known. Besides, we have two wonderful children as a result of your efforts." That simple fact put it all in perspective.

Meanwhile, I can still rest on several laurels. Jenny and David just celebrated their thirtieth wedding anniversary with a luxury cruise on the Mediterranean, their dream vacation. Their daughters are grown and out of the house, and they are enjoying their status as empty nesters. Jenny has become my dear friend, serving as matron of honor at Jim's and my wedding. I have had a front row seat to the ups and downs of their journey together. Through it all, they remain hopelessly in love. Every year on their anniversary, Jenny looks forward to David's annual recitation of the tale of how they met and fell in love. He draws out the narrative, describing how she "reeled him in" complete with fishing pole gesticulations and sound effects. David's performance is far better than any gift she could ask for, although his most recent gift of an extravagant diamond anniversary ring came awfully close.

Rhonda, who was widowed from Leo, re-engaged my services in her seventies and was fortunate to experience a three-month relationship with Mason, a man in his early eighties whom I introduced to her, and who quickly fell head over heels for her. While she enjoyed the attention and the intimacy between them, she ultimately decided that he was not the man for her. It did, however, serve as a reminder to her that even at her age, it's possible to experience a romantic spark as powerfully as ever.

Jackie, who had been so devastated by Pablo's rejection, is now deeply in love with Eddie, whom I recruited from an affiliate matchmaker. Although they are challenged by the geographic distance between them, they have both committed to doing everything in their power to maintain their communication and to meet as often as possible. They have met each other's children, as well as each other's closest friends. Recently, she expressed her feelings that despite their previous marriages and divorces, they both feel that they have been waiting all their lives to be together.

Jim and I continue to learn and practice the skills of being married to each other, which is a life lesson we both work at yet cherish. Jim already knew how to be a good husband but is learning what being a good husband to *me* actually means. As a matchmaker who is finally in the marriage I always aspired to, this journey is tremendously gratifying. Every March 10, the anniversary of our first date at Founding Farmers, we re-enact the experience by meeting at the bar where we first laid eyes on each other in March 2012. This annual ritual reminds us how fortunate we are and is a testament to the magic that can occur between even the most unlikely matches. On the night we met, neither of us would have ever imagined that we would end up happily married, yet it miraculously happened.

The romantic in me continues to put people together, to take risks, and to learn from each interaction, whether positive or negative. Every day, I count my blessings, cross my fingers, put one foot in front of the other, and ask the universe to deliver.

# ABOUT THE AUTHOR

*L*eora Kusher Hoffman was born in Israel and raised in Brooklyn, New York. After graduating law school in 1982, she lived and worked in London, England, before moving to Washington, DC, where she began her career as a practicing attorney in the field of criminal defense and civil litigation.

In 1986, Leora joined the Commodity Futures Trading Commission, where she served as an attorney in the trading and markets division. After the birth of her second child three years later, she left the federal government to start her matchmaking business, focusing on professional singles in the Washington DC/Baltimore area.

In 1999, Leora established a private law practice in the field of child protection in DC family court, representing children in the neglect system. While concurrently running her matchmaking business, Leora joined the Office of the Attorney General of DC in 2003 and served as an assistant attorney general in the Child Protection Division, where she served until 2015 when she left the legal profession to expand her matchmaking company.

Leora is a frequent public speaker in the area of relationships and matchmaking and has appeared on public, cable, and network TV as well as public radio and podcasts. She has been featured in numerous newspaper and magazine articles including *Washingtonian* magazine, *The Washington Post, Washington Jewish Week, The Washington Times,* and *The Baltimore Sun.*

Leora currently specializes in the fifty plus demographic. Over her thirty plus years in business, she has been responsible for seventy-six marriages and hundreds of long-term relationships. She currently resides in Garrett Park, Maryland, a Washington, DC, suburb, with her husband Jim.

Made in the USA
Columbia, SC
03 February 2020